The Courtship

of

Sarah McLean

The Courtship

of

Sarah McLean

By Mr. and Mrs. Stephen B. Castleberry

Castleberry Farms Press

First Edition
© Copyright 1996
Castleberry Farms Press
P.O. Box 337
Poplar, WI 54864

ISBN 1-886028-16-8
Library of Congress Catalog Card Number: 96-067747

Published in cooperation with:
Savage Press

Printed in the U.S.A.

Cover art was created by:
Jeffrey T. Larson, Maple, Wisconsin

A Note From the Authors

Believing that God looks on the heart and not on outward appearances, we purposefully have avoided describing Sarah's physical characteristics, as well as those of the other characters. We want to encourage ourselves as well as other Christians to see people not as the world sees them, but as God sees them.

> "But the Lord said unto Samuel, Look not on his countenance, or on the height of his stature; because I have refused him: for the Lord seeth not as man seeth; for man looketh on the outward appearance, but the Lord looketh on the heart." I Samuel 16:7

We sincerely hope you will enjoy reading *The Courtship of Sarah McLean*. It is our intention, if it is God's will, to offer a number of other books on courtship as well as general reading materials for boys (such as a farm mystery series that does not contain murders or objectionable material). Our primary goal in publishing is to provide wholesome books for Christian families in a manner that brings honor to our Lord. We always welcome your comments, suggestions and, most importantly, your prayers.

If you would like to hear about upcoming titles you can reach us at this address:

Mr. and Mrs. Stephen B. Castleberry
Castleberry Farms Press
P.O. Box 337
Poplar, WI 54864

Chapter One

*S*arah glanced absently out of the window as she stirred the cookie dough. It was such a beautiful, warm morning and, with the windows open wide, she was able to hear the bluebirds singing sweetly in the lilac bush outside. Spring. Sarah loved all of the seasons because they brought such different things to do and see. But spring had always awakened something in her that she couldn't quite explain. It was as if the world was coming alive again.

Rachel, her little five-year-old sister who was helping make the cookies, broke Sarah's train of thought: "Did you remember to add that white stuff out of the big can? Once Mommy forgot and the cookies didn't taste right."

Sarah looked over at her little sister and smiled. Rachel's sparkling blue eyes and sweet, chubby cheeks made her the joy of the family. Her spirit was as joyful as her face and she was a pleasure to have around when one was doing any task. Today, Sarah was extra glad for her happy chatter and eager questions.

Sarah had been feeling a little sad the last few days, without really knowing why. It seemed that she could say with Paul the apostle that she was perplexed but not in despair. But why did she even feel downcast? Why should she? Her loving family supplied plenty of activity and laughter. With three brothers and

9

three sisters, what more could she want?

Becky, her three-year-old sister, was known for her easy laughter and little acts of kindness. Why, just this morning Becky had surprised her by making Sarah's bed and putting her clothes away. Of course the fact that the clothes were actually dirty and should have been put in the hamper instead of Sarah's drawer didn't matter. And the bed, . . . well, the bed didn't look made, but Becky sure thought it did!

Then there was Steve, a fireball of a brother at eight years of age. Steve never stopped. He played hard, worked hard, ran hard, and slept hard. Sarah felt so blessed to have a little brother who loved to run and fetch things for her. She knew it made him feel grown up when she asked for his help or advice. A couple of days ago she had asked his opinion about a new dress she had just finished making. You could tell by his smile that he felt so grown-up to be giving his nineteen-year-old sister advice. "I think you've done a fine job," he said, trying his best to sound like Dad.

Of course Ben was also a part of Sarah's loving family. Ben was her quiet, almost shy, brother who was ten and a half years-old. He seemed to live for being in the outdoors, usually playing with his BB gun. Although he was never unkind, he was noticeably reserved. When most people in the family were just sitting around talking or playing games, if anyone was missing, it was usually Ben. It was hard for people to know what Ben was thinking or feeling, and Sarah was no better at figuring him out than anyone else.

Fourteen-year-old Janet was the member of the family who most enjoyed being with other families.

All the neighbors appreciated Janet, who was always willing to help out when needed. The negative side of this was that Janet tended to think more highly of other families than she did of her own. She was often heard to say something like, "Well, I wish we could . . . like the Johns do . . ."

Jeff, the oldest boy in the family, had just turned seventeen three weeks ago. Although he was almost an adult, he still enjoyed playing with his brothers and sisters. Sarah especially enjoyed taking walks with him. Their walks had resulted in many interesting talks over the years, about what they believed and about their future. Jeff was just sure he was going to be a farmer and loved to share his dreams with his oldest sister. He never had to preface his conversations with "Now, don't tell anyone this . . . " because he obviously considered Sarah his closest confidant.

Mom was a helpful, quiet friend who always had time for Sarah and her questions. While some of the other girls Sarah's age had talked disrespectfully about their mothers at times, Sarah had never done so about Mom. She just couldn't. Everyone, even people outside her family, knew Mom to be a committed follower of Jesus Christ. Sure, she wasn't perfect. But Mom was willing to admit her mistakes and ask forgiveness of whomever she had hurt. She was certainly a role model for Sarah!

And then there was Dad. The man who had taught her so much about living a Christian life. He seemed to always know when to be funny, or when to be serious. Dad was kind to both man and beast. He didn't want to hurt anyone or anything. Yet he had certainly taken his responsibility in discipline seriously. When Dad had to punish one of the children, it was obvious that he did so with love and firmness. Hugs and smiles always followed these episodes.

Little Rachel broke into Sarah's thoughts again, and she realized her sister had been chattering about the Larsons' new baby. "Mrs. Larson let me hold baby Matt on my lap after church yesterday. He is so sweet and tiny and new. Babies are special, aren't they Sarah? Why is that?"

Sarah smiled down at Rachel's upturned eyes, so filled with questioning wonder. "God made them that way, Rachel. Maybe it is to remind us to take good care of them for Him. And maybe it helps us remember that Jesus said we must be like little children to enter the kingdom of Heaven."

Rachel was suddenly quiet for a minute, thinking over what her big sister had said. "Well, I sure love babies. I can hardly wait until I'm a mommy. Sarah, when will you be a mommy?"

Sarah paused for a moment, her spoon suspended in mid-air. Suddenly she knew the cause of her inner discontent. She was happy at home and trusted her parents' decisions. She had been delighted when her parents decided that courtship was God's will for their children instead of dating. But now . . . well, now she had just turned nineteen. And no one had asked to court her yet. She didn't know if anyone was even interested in her. How Sarah longed for the day when she could have a husband, home, and children of her own. How eagerly she looked forward to the day when a tiny, sweet, new baby in her arms would be her own.

Sarah was ready in so many ways. Dad simply raved when she cooked the evening meal. That couldn't be just Dad being nice, because even Ben commented on how good her cooking was! After years of struggling with a touch of laziness in her cleaning, Sarah felt that she had finally learned to accept cleaning the house as something she should do well—"as unto the Lord." Although she was too humble to speak of it, her sewing skills were also top notch. She could make just about anything with a pattern, and even many things without a pattern. As for taking care of children and even small babies, hadn't she been helping Mom for the last ten years or so? Why, she had changed diapers, helped potty train toddlers, rocked sick children, bandaged cuts and scrapes, and helped resolve disputes more times than she could count. Yes, she felt that she was ready to be married in so many ways. But was there more for her to learn before God said she was ready? Was there some reason she had no young man courting her?

Chapter Two

*S*everal weeks went by. Weeks in which Sarah thought a good bit about marriage. Oh, she didn't try to. It just kept popping, unbidden, into her head. Early Sunday, her family went through its usual Sunday morning rushing around to get ready to attend church. It seemed almost a foregone conclusion that Steve was going to get messed up somehow between the time he got dressed and the time his family walked out the door! Today was no exception. He had only been trying to help. The cows did need more water, didn't they? How did he know he was going to fall while running out of the barn? After Sarah helped find another pair of pants and Steve made a quick change, the family hurried out of the house.

As Sarah was sitting in church, she felt less rushed. Funny how that worked. Going to church almost always started a comforting feeling inside her. It was, in some strange way, as though she were home. Church strengthened, encouraged, and motivated her to live her life more in conformance to the will of her Savior. Of course, that didn't mean that her mind never wandered. At times she would be sitting there, listening intently to the sermon, only to "wake up" a few minutes later and realize that she was thinking about something that had nothing to do with church (like how to get a stain out of her new dress, or planning a

14

conversation she was going to have with a friend tomorrow). She wondered if it only happened to her, and was too embarrassed to ask her mom about it. She was just sure it showed a lack of spiritual maturity to let it happen.

This Sunday as the sermon was begun, though, she felt sure she wouldn't be daydreaming. The preacher had begun with these words: "Today, I would like to talk about what God's desire for marriage is. This teaching is for everyone present today, but perhaps is even more relevant to those of you who have not yet entered God's blessed state of matrimony." Sarah grabbed her pencil and notebook (she tried to remember to take notes of the sermons each week, and study them later in the day) and took a deep breath. Perhaps this sermon is just what she needed to hear. After prayer, the pastor continued.

"Marriage is a most important institution, and was designed by God to bring further glory and honor to Himself. God didn't leave man in the dark about this institution, though, and has provided us with many directives about how to get married, as well as how to live in the married state. Sadly, local custom often has more influence than God's Word. The custom that has evolved in our culture today is that a young person generally dates a number of people, and then decides whom he or she will marry, based on the experiences and knowledge learned from these dates. No doubt some of you here probably followed that path in your own life. And you probably know people who are dating even today. What does God's Word say about dating? Is it okay? Is it sinful? Is there a better way?

Let's take a look.

"First, let me state clearly that the words 'date' and 'dating' are not found in scriptures. Neither is 'courting.' Before you dismiss the topic as having no Biblical references, however, you need to note that many things are not specifically mentioned in the Bible, yet God has revealed His will. For example, taking illegal drugs or watching an x-rated movie are never mentioned in the Bible. Yet we have many scriptures which remind us that our bodies are the temple of God and that we are to honor them as such.

"The underlying concern that most Christians have with the casual dating occurring in our culture today is the lack of purity it can allow and even encourage. God's Word says in I Timothy 5:22 to ' . . . keep thyself pure.' Philippians 4:8 echoes this command by stating, 'Finally, brethren, whatsoever things are true, whatsoever things are honest, whatsoever things are just, whatsoever things are pure, whatsoever things are lovely, whatsoever things are of good report; if there be any virtue, and if there be any praise, think on these things.' We are to abstain from even the appearance of evil so that we might be a light unto the world as I Thessalonians 5:22, Philippians 2:15, and many other verses command us."

The preacher adjusted his notes a little and continued. "God has given specific instructions and commands about purity for His followers. I Thessalonians 4:3-5, 7 clearly reveals God's will. It states, 'For this is the will of God, even your sanctification, that ye should abstain from fornication: that every one of you should know how to possess his vessel in sanctification and honor; not in lust of concupiscence, even as the Gentiles which know not God: . . . For God hath not called us unto uncleanness, but unto holiness.' Again, there are many other passages which reveal the same command. Ephesians 5:3 states, 'But fornication, and all uncleanness, or covetousness, let it not be once named among you, as becometh saints.'

It is in the context of purity that dating can be very dangerous. Dating leads to many opportunities for Satan to tempt you. A young man and young woman alone, often at night, on a date, have no accountability. No one knows where they are, what they say, what they do. With courtship, all of this is avoided. The real purpose of finding God's will for a marriage partner can be accomplished in a pure and wholesome way, with no later regrets.

Another advantage of courtship over dating is that it helps to focus the attention of the relationship on truly discovering the character and Christian maturity of the potential mate. Thisis aided in courtship by the active involvement of both sets of parents. With the wisdom supplied by the Holy Spirit, parents can help their children avoid marriages that are not in God's will. Let's face it. Too often, young people can get so wrapped up emotionally in a relationship that they cannot clearly evaluate the other person objectively. Parents can help. For example, a girl's parents can help ensure that their daughter does not become unequally yoked with a nonbeliever, something that 2 Corinthians 6:14 clearly commands Christians to avoid.

In casual dating, by contrast, the focus is usually on having fun and getting to seriously know lots of different members of the opposite sex. Marriage is often the farthest thought from the dating person's mind. This cavalier attitude can actually result in one ultimately taking marriage less seriously. If a young man, for example, can sample a lot of different relationships before marriage, why not start sampling again after he is married and bored with his wife? All too often, I'm afraid that is exactly what is happening in our land today. Commitment, courtship, and seriousness have been replaced with no commitments, dating, and entertainment.

"Of everyone I have ever talked with on this subject, all those who dated had some regrets, some things they wish had never happened." The preacher shifted a little and looked down at his Bible. It seemed as if what he was going to say next was particularly hard for him. "Yes, it's even true for me. I must admit to you who don't already know this, that I dated before I married Ruth, my lovely wife of 35 years. Everyone I knew at that time also dated, and I wasn't even aware that there was any other way to learn about potential marriage partners. And even though I did end up marrying Ruth, for which I am eternally thankful to God, it did leave some problems in our marriage that we have had to work out through the years. For example, even after 35 years, it is still a little painful to think that Ruth had several steady boyfriends that she dated for a long time. She shared her thoughts and dreams with them in a way that should have been reserved for her future husband alone. I also used to wonder if she was sizing me up and comparing me to some of her earlier beaus. Was I not as smart, not as witty, not as handsome as some of her former loves, I used to wonder? Was she really satisfied with me, or did she wish she could have dated a little more, and sampled a few others' wit and intelligence before settling down? I'm afraid I was pretty jealous those first few years of our married life. Even though she didn't often bring up the issue of her former boyfriends, I knew they were there in her mind. Frankly, all of my jealousy and worry could have been avoided.

Oh, what if it had been different? What if it had been like this: As a young man I prayed to God for direction in choosing my life's partner and mate. My future spouse, Ruth, did the same thing. As God led me, I learned more about Ruth. After much prayer and counsel from my parents, I talked to Ruth's father. I shared with him my belief that Ruth might be who God had chosen for me to marry and my seriousness in desiring to explore that possibility. After we prayed, I left and he talked it over with his wife and prayed some more. Finally, after considering what he knew of my Christian maturity and my seriousness, he talked to Ruth. After prayer, Ruth also decided she would like me to court her. So over the next several months, Ruth and I met, always in the company of her family, and talked and got to know each other better. After several months, I asked Ruth's father if I could marry her. He had many opportunities to talk with me and observe me over the last several months and, with prayer, he agreed to let Ruth marry me. Imagine my joy the night I finally proposed to Ruth in this scenario and she accepted. It is a scenario I wish was actual history in my life. It can be for you. Pray that God would direct you in the paths He has chosen for you.

Is courting the only godly way to gain a spouse? I believe it is something like what an Amishman once told me. He said, 'I do not believe that the Amish way of life is the plan of salvation. I do believe that it is a real help to me in living in conformance to God's will.' In the same way, courtship is not the plan of salvation! But courtship is a real help to young unmarried people, trying to live their lives in accordance with God's will."

As the preacher concluded his sermon, Sarah was left with a resolve to follow God's will for her life in the area of courting. The pastor's story had been very moving, and she had placed herself in Ruth's place, as he was talking. Oh, it was possible! And it really could happen. Maybe even soon. She had a little spring in her step as she walked away with her family.

Arriving home, however, Sarah found herself just a little discontented again. It's sad the way the devil can take away your joy if you're not careful. What if no one courted her? What if no one wanted to marry her? She knew this was possible because she knew unmarried women who wished to be married. Martha, a woman in Sarah's community, was one of these women. In fact, if anything, Sarah would characterize Martha as quite bitter about not being married.

Would Sarah be bitter if the same thing happened to her? She prayed that she would not. After all, the apostle Paul stated in Philippians 4:11: ". . . for I have learned, in whatsoever state I am, therewith to be content." Above all things, she really did want to be content and please God with her thoughts and her life. As she went to sleep that night, she prayed: "God, help me to trust in you. Help me to wait for the man you may want to send to me. And please help me to remain committed to courtship. Your will be done."

Chapter Three

The sun was beginning to rise a little later and set a little earlier each day. Sarah's family stayed busy, it seemed, from morning till night, gathering crops, putting away last fields of hay, picking and canning vegetables, and gathering firewood. Oh, but she wasn't complaining. Sarah loved fall. She loved to sit by the window and watch squirrels busily gathering nuts for the winter. In the same way, it was comforting to her to see God's provision of food for their family for the winter, and be able to be a part of its harvest. Of course, her back ached sometimes from stooping over too much and her hands got all stained from the many vegetables and fruits she canned. Yet, she was thankful. She thought the pantry shelves full of jars filled with wonderful foods such as jams, fruits, corn and pumpkin were beautiful to look at.

It was also neat the way the whole family pitched in and worked together in a way that other seasons just didn't require. Becky, who often had trouble finding something useful to do, could actually be of help as she washed and rinsed vegetables. The work brought a sense of camaraderie and closeness that included even Ben.

It was on a cool Monday morning during this season that Mom called Jeff and Sarah to her. "We're going to need some more apples. I want you two to run down to the market and bring home a bushel of good tart apples we can use to make applesauce. Here's some money. Now, do try and get back soon. I'd like to get most of the applesauce finished today, if at all possible." As her children left the house, Mom watched them walk down the road. No, she wasn't worried about their safety. Even though Jeff was only seventeen, he was already built like a farmer. His strong hands and stocky build seemed to keep anyone from ever thinking of bothering them.

As they neared the market, Jeff said, "Do you think we can get some Jonathan apples this time? I really like them better than the Winesap for applesauce." Sarah was feeling pretty good that day, and decided to have a little fun. Answering as though Jeff were a little boy shopping with his mother, she stated: "Well, we'll just have to see what they have available, won't we Jeffy? Mother doesn't know how much each one costs, either. We'll just have to see, Jeffy," Sarah replied, smiling at her brother. Her tone of voice was intended to mimic a mother's and Jeff caught on right away that he was to act the part of a small boy, pleading with his mother. "Oh, please! Please! Can't I have some? Pleasssseeeee?" appealed Jeff, almost laughing out loud from playing the part of a little boy. To finish his act he gave Sarah a hug, and looked into her face with puppy dog eyes, just as he had seen little children beg their mothers at the market.

Across the market, Tim Jones was watching this exchange with not a little interest. He had noticed Sarah at the market many times before and had been attracted to her, although he didn't really know anything about her. "Believe she's already spoken for, Tim," a voice half-whispered from behind. Was it that obvious that Tim was interested? Tim turned, and saw one of his fellow employees, George, looking in the direction of Sarah.

"What do you mean?" Tim asked. "You know exactly what I mean, Tim old boy," said George. "Every time that young lady enters this market you seem to forget that anyone or anything else exists. Don't you think I can see what's going on?"

"Well, what if I do notice her? Is there any law against that?" growled Tim. Although Tim wouldn't admit it, he had an explosive temper and frequent bouts of anger.

"Back off! Back off, Tim!" said George. "I was merely making a statement that might save your neck. From the size of that guy's arms, I'd be pretty careful how interested I seemed in that girl. Didn't you see him give her a hug?"

"No, you're all wrong, as usual," said Tim, cooling off a little. "I've seen him in here before with her and heard her tell another shopper that he was her brother. But..." he said, noticing the size of Jeff's arms for the first time, "I will keep your advice in mind. I'll bet he is pretty protective of her."

"Well, if you want to get to know her better, why not ask her out for a date?" asked George. "There's no better way to get to know a girl, and besides you might have fun in the process."

"I don't know. I'll have to think about it, I guess," said Tim.

That was the end of their conversation because

Tim walked away and started moving toward Sarah and her brother. As he did so, he consciously tried to remove any semblance of anger that might still be lurking on his face.

"Can I help you, ma'am?" Tim asked, talking to Sarah, but keeping an eye on Jeff.

"Yes, we're looking to buy some good tart apples for making applesauce," replied Sarah. "Are these Jonathan apples new crop? I mean are they fresh from this year, or are they stored apples from a previous season?"

"Oh, they're this season's apples all right," Tim said. "We just got them in yesterday. Would you like to try a bite?" he asked, picking up a nice red one.

"If that would be okay, yes," Sarah answered. It was fresh all right, and pretty tart, too. She noticed that Tim was looking at her kind of funny as she tasted the apple. Why? she wondered. She had assumed that he was serious when he said it was okay to taste an apple. Was he worried about her eating an apple without buying it first? Maybe she was just imagining things, however, because now Tim was talking to Jeff. She picked up on their conversation.

"Yeah, I've been working here about a year now," Tim was saying. "It's a pretty good job. You wouldn't believe the different kinds of people you get to meet! Some are pretty weird. But making money is what I like best about this job! It does eat up most of my free time, though."

"I'm sure it does. But working hard is something we might as well get used to," Jeff added. "We're going to be doing it the rest of our lives. Right Sarah?"

25

"I imagine so," answered Sarah.

Turning his full attention to Sarah, Tim said, "I guess making applesauce is pretty hard work too?" After Sarah answered, he continued to talk to Sarah and seemed to have nothing else to do.

After a few minutes, Sarah said to Jeff, "Well, I guess we'd better be getting these apples home so Mom can start making applesauce. Goodbye,...ah... "

"Tim's my name," was Tim's quick reply.

Tim wished he could ask Sarah for a date right now. Why, he could even invite her to go with him to the concert this weekend. But he sure wouldn't ask her with Sarah's brother right there listening to the whole thing! No, he would just have to wait until sometime when Sarah was alone. He knew his time would come sooner or later.

Tim kept thinking about Sarah as he worked the rest of the day. What did he know abouther? He knew she was a religious person because she always wore some kind of a covering on top of her head, like many of the church ladies who came in. He had also seen her talking to the preacher in the market on several occasions. Tim had never been to church, although he considered himself as good as those church people. In fact, he was proud that he was better than many of those hypocrites who went to church. How many times he had seen someone who claimed to be a Christian do things they weren't supposed to do! Just today, he was pretty sure he saw one of those ladies with a covering on her head slyly slide a bar of candy into her purse to avoid having to pay for it. The nerve! And if you ever gave them back too much change or forgot to charge them for something, did these Christians tell you? Not on your life. As Tim thought about it, he realized that he was actually much more honest and good than most of the Christians he had met.

On the way home from the market, Jeff commented, "Tim sure seemed awfully friendly. Even though I just met him and don't know him well, he seemed to be in unusually good spirits when he was talking to you. Better be careful, Sarah!"

"What do you mean, Jeff?" Sarah asked. "He just talked to us a little. Do you think he said anything wrong?"

Jeff laughed. "Oh, no, everything was fine. I guess I just don't want anyone getting too friendly with you. I know someday you'll get married and leave us, but, well . . . I guess I'm not really looking forward to it. It will have to be somebody pretty special to seem good enough for you."

Sarah smiled and squeezed his arm. "Thanks, Jeff. You're a pretty special brother, yourself," she noted.

Chapter Four

*T*im didn't have to wait as long as he feared. Just two weeks later, Sarah, without Jeff, entered the market to do some shopping. Without trying to seem obvious, Tim slowly moved across the market so that Sarah would cross his path as she shopped. When she did, Tim looked up and said, "Hi! How did the apples work out? Pretty good applesauce I guess?"

Sarah smiled, "Yes, it was pretty good apple sauce, but we won't be tasting most of it until the dead of winter you know. I hope I didn't get you into any kind of trouble by tasting that free apple you offered?"

"No, of course not," Tim answered. "Our market has a policy that allows a customer to taste the produce, especially if they are thinking of buying in fairly large quantities. Say," he continued, trying to move ahead before he lost his courage, "there's going to be a hay ride at the farm of one of my neighbors, this Saturday night. They're really nice people, too. It'll just last about two hours and they're planning on having a hot dog roast by a campfire. Would you like to come with me?" He was glad that he had gotten it out, although it seemed a little awkward to be asking her this, right next to a huge display of squash.

For a moment, Sarah just stood looking at the squash. She honestly didn't know what to say. All of her prayers, her conversations with her parents and friends, and her dreams had not included something like this. She didn't think someone would just ask her for a date. What should she say? What should she do now? Is Tim even a Christian? If he is a Christian, couldn't God be using this somehow to start her courtship? Sarah struggled with her thoughts and emotions. It was the first time a young man had so obviously shown a strong liking for her. She so wanted it to work out!

After a few very awkward moments, she looked up into Tim's eyes. Hurt is all she saw there. She supposed that her long interval of thinking had made him nervous and then, a little bit angry. After all, if she was interested, wouldn't she have answered right away? The way it was, it looked as if she was trying to think of a polite way to tell him no. The truth was that she was not ready to close any doors right now. Sarah didn't really know Tim, but what if this was who God had chosen for her? She felt like she needed to give that a chance.

Finally, she started mumbling, "Well, . . . I'm sure your neighbors are nice . . . but, Saturday, . . . dating, instead of courtship, well, . . . I do like campfires . . ." What was wrong with her? For nineteen years she had never been accused of having trouble talking! So why couldn't she talk to this nice young man right now? Sarah quickly prayed silently to God to give her wisdom and the right words to say.

Tim was getting more agitated every second. He shuffled around and looked to see who was watching this ordeal. Oh great! It looked like George was smiling to himself over on the other side of the market.

He probably figured out what was happening and would never let Tim live this down. Well, Tim would sure set him straight in a hurry!

Sarah surprised herself by suddenly saying out loud, "Thanks for asking me, Tim, but I'm afraid that just isn't possible." She had said it softly and kindly. "Now, I'm afraid I need to finish my shopping because my mom is waiting for these mushrooms for the lunch she is preparing. Good-bye, Tim." Sarah moved away and thanked God for giving her the words to say. She hoped that she had not hurt Tim's feelings.

As she turned to head home, thoughts started swirling in her mind. Why was it so hard to turn down a date? She knew that casual dating wasn't God's plan for her life, so why had she hesitated? Oh, she knew all right, she was just trying to think of good excuses for her hesitancy. The truth was that she was very pleased that a young man had taken an interest in her! It was something she had longed for and prayed for. And then, when someone showed an interest, she had trouble saying "no." She knew dating Tim was not the answer to her many prayers. Not only was dating wrong for her, but she simply didn't know anything about Tim. Who were his parents? What did he believe? What were his character traits? Would he be willing to go through a courtship, even though he apparently didn't know much about how it worked? As she neared her house, she whispered a prayer, "May Your will be done." Suddenly she felt some of her burden being lifted.

Tim also experienced questions and thoughts after Sarah left. He felt exposed and humiliated. Why couldn't she just say "yes," or even "no?" After all, she wasn't a little kid! The other girls that he had dated sure didn't act like she had just acted. They had always been able to make decisions quickly. The more he thought about it the more angry he became. He was walking into the storeroom at this moment, and his foot brushed a box lying there. Without hesitation he kicked the box as hard as he could, sending it sailing into a pile of milk crates stacked up against the wall. Those crates then came tumbling down and made an awful racket. "Who cares!" growled Tim.

It was then that he noticed George in one corner of the storeroom watching Tim's behavior. "She said 'no,' didn't she?" George asked. "I'm sorry for you. I know it's no fun. Hey, don't let it get you down, okay? There are always more girls in this world."

"Oh, leave me alone!" Tim shouted. "What makes you think you know everything?"

"I didn't mean anything, Tim, honest," George replied. "I was just trying to make you feel better. Look, you're a sharp guy and there are lots of girls that would probably like to date you. Why, I happen to know that Judy here at the market has been interested in you for some time. Why not ask her for that date?"

"If I wanted your advice I would have asked for it!" Tim shouted again. It was obvious that his lifelong problem with anger and resentment was still with him. He had recognized that he was an angry person early in his life, but had never seen any reason to change it. In fact, he used it to get his way many times. Most people had been willing to do anything to get Tim to stop being angry at them. Sometimes a man just had to be good and angry, or at least he thought so. And this was one of those times!

As the day wore on, Tim calmed down more. He was finally able to see that Sarah had said nothing to hurt him on purpose. In fact, she had been very careful to not hurt his feelings. And the more he thought about it the more he realized that he really wanted to get to know Sarah better. There was something about her, though he didn't know exactly what, that attracted him to her. "Maybe she's going to be the one for me," he thought to himself.

At one point in that day, Tim worked near Judy. He remembered what George had said about Judy wanting to date him. Judy seemed like a very nice girl, and Tim couldn't understand why, but he didn't feel like dating her. The more he thought about it, the more he realized that he was comparing her to Sarah. But what did he really know about Sarah anyway? Except for watching her and talking to her at the market occasionally, he realized he didn't know that much about her. She seemed to be playing hard to get. Well, if that was the way she wanted to play this game, he could play along. It was sure worth a try. Tim smiled as he headed back to the produce section. "I'll just have to keep trying," he whispered as he straightened the lettuce.

Chapter Five

Thanksgiving had always been one of Sarah's favorite holidays. For as long as she could remember, her family had done the same things, and she delighted in knowing that those traditions would be continued every year. The week before Thanksgiving, she and Mom seemed to spend hours reading Pilgrim stories to the younger children. From the persecution of the Separatists, through the Mayflower voyage, to the Thanksgiving feast, everything had to be explained over and over again.

Janet helped Steve, Rachel, and Becky make turkeys on construction paper using their spread-out hands for a pattern, then adding a beak and wattle to the thumb for a head, and coloring the fingers as feathers. Ben was eleven now, and made his own elaborate turkey from construction paper and some genuine turkey feathers he had saved from September's butchering. Mom showed the little ones how to color paper bags to look like Indian costumes, and cut fringe along the bottom edge of the bag. After cutting arm holes and a hole for the head, she slit the bag up the front, so that it was easy to get off and on little arms.

Finally, Thanksgiving day arrived, with all of the spicy, sweet smells that Sarah so well remembered. Over all seemed to drift the aroma of the roasting turkey. Sarah set the table with Great-Grandmother's china and let Rachel and Becky put out the napkins and silver. Janet ran up and down the basement steps for Mom several times, fetching ingredients for all the special foods they enjoyed. Fortunately, Sarah, Mom, and Janet had prepared ahead all that they possibly could the day before Thanksgiving, so that when they sat down to dinner, they truly felt thankful and cheerful, instead of hot and tired.

After the blessing, Dad served the turkey while Mom helped Becky and Rachel to all the other food. Everyone had a good appetite from smelling the food cooking all morning and Sarah was no exception. They all had second helpings of something, but they weren't allowed to stuff themselves, even at Thanksgiving. Mom always said that being gluttonous didn't seem like a good way to show the Lord a thankful spirit.

When most of them had finished, and the younger children were still eating their pie, Dad began their favorite tradition. That morning he had cut many strips of paper for everyone to use, and each member of the family had written (or someone had helped them write) several things for which they were thankful. They also had signed each slip, then folded them and placed them in a basket. Now Dad unfolded each one and read them aloud as everyone listened, often smiling and nodding in agreement. Sometimes one of the little girls would excitedly add, "Oh, me too! I'm thankful for that, too!" The topics were always varied, and seemed to cover almost everything. For example, one of Rachel's slips read, "I'm thankful for sunshine and butterflies in the summertime." One of Jeff's read, "I am thankful for walks with Sarah." There were literally dozens of them.

When Dad had finished reading, Sarah realized that as varied as the slips were, they only touched a tiny portion of all that God had given them to be thankful for. Placing the last slip back into the basket, Dad smiled at his family. Then he reached over and held Mom's hand, who sat on a bench beside his chair at the head of the table.

"We all truly have been blessed by God this year, as we have been every year. And today, Mom and I want to share with you something that we are especially thankful for. God has blessed us with the hope of another new little life. Lord willing, you will have another brother or sister next summer."

All the McLean children looked in wide-eyed delight and astonishment at Mom. She had often spoken of hoping God would send another baby, but Becky was almost four, and Sarah knew that Mom was trying to accept the fact that Becky might always be the youngest of her children. Surprisingly, it was Ben who spoke first.

"Mom, how great! God has given us the best Thanksgiving ever, hasn't He?"

"He surely has, Ben," Mom smiled over at him, with tears in her eyes. "He surely has."

Then Dad bowed his head and prayed, thanking God for all His many blessings, especially the new baby.

"In honor of the new baby," Jeff announced, "I think Mom should take a nap this afternoon while the rest of us clean the kitchen."

"Even Dad?" asked Steve. "Dad never cleans

the kitchen!"

"Oh, I wouldn't say never," laughed Dad. "I would just say that I usually respect Mom and Sarah's superior abilities in the kitchen. But today, I'll help too. In fact," Dad continued, "while we work, I'll tell you about what Thanksgiving was like at my house when I was growing up."

"Oh goody, a story!" Becky exclaimed in delight. "I just love Daddy's stories!"

"Then maybe I should tell you two stories. But first," suggested Dad, "how about you and Rachel washing that pumpkin pie off your faces? Then we'll get started. Up to bed, Mom," he directed with a smile.

Later that night, after evening family devotions, Mom took Steve, Rachel and Becky upstairs to read them a chapter of a book after they were tucked in bed. This was a regular routine for them, and no one dawdled about getting into bed, for fear of missing even one sentence of the story. Ben and Jeff worked on a jigsaw puzzle together, and Dad spoke quietly to Sarah and Janet. "Girls, let's go into the kitchen for a few minutes. Why don't you make us some hot chocolate, Janet? Then I'd like to talk to you both."

Dad laughed at the girls' curious expressions. "Don't worry, you're not in any trouble," he assured them. "I just need to ask you for your help in something important." They both gave him a relieved smile, and Janet hurried to make the steaming cups of chocolate.

When they were seated at the table, Dad stirred the hot liquid slowly and thoughtfully. Then looking at each of his oldest daughters, he began, "You know girls, this new little life is such a wonderful surprise. Mom and I had both pretty much given up hoping for another child, but God knew all along that He would be giving us this baby. Of course, we don't know how long we will be given the privilege of having it be a part of our family."

Dad paused for a moment and Sarah knew he was silently remembering the two babies Mom had miscarried, one a year before Rachel was born, and the other just two years ago. Dad cleared his throat, then continued. "No matter what He has planned, we know He is good and we are thankful for the hope He has given us. But girls," Dad looked seriously at them, "we need to keep in mind that we have a job to do now. Mom is getting older, you know. She will be 42 in just a few weeks. That isn't ancient of course, and many women have had babies who are even a few years older than Mom. But it is very important that she be able to rest a lot throughout this pregnancy, and that she has as little strain on her as possible. You are both certainly a big help to her and we appreciate that. However, there are still many things that I think we can change around here to make it even easier on her, if we put our heads together. You are actually able to do pretty much everything Mom does, and I think it would be best to take over anything and everything that Mom will let you."

Sarah nodded eagerly. "I know we could, Dad. But she always likes to do certain things herself. I don't want to be bossy - Mom would sure never stand for that! What should we do?"

"Well," Dad grinned, "That's where I come in.

Mom stands for me being bossy pretty well, doesn't she? She has become a truly submissive wife over the years, and I know she'll let me decide what is best. Now get me some paper and a pen and we'll decide what needs to be changed for the next few months."

Sarah, Janet, and their father thought of quite a few things that could be changed, including Sarah taking over all the cooking until Mom was over her nausea. "I know what you mean about Mom liking to do certain things herself," Dad laughed, as they discussed Sarah's cooking responsibilities. "We knew about the baby a few days ago and Mom has already felt sick several times, but she really wanted to surprise everyone on Thanksgiving with the news. I'm sure cooking Thanksgiving dinner wasn't exactly a pleasant task this morning, but she was determined!"

Sarah laughed too, then spoke up with a new idea. "Let's get the little girls involved, too, Dad. It will make them so happy to feel they are helping more. They already have a couple of small jobs, but could we come up with a few new ones? We could keep them really easy, of course, but I think they would be very pleased to be helping take care of the baby already, even before it is born."

"That's great," agreed Dad. "What do you have in mind?" A few minutes later, everything seemed to be settled. As they got up to rinse their cups at the sink, Mom, Jeff, and Ben walked into the kitchen.

"Hey Mom, can you make us some popcorn?" asked Jeff.

"That sounds good, Mom! Please?" added Ben. "I have 30 minutes left before I have to go to bed. I'm sure I can eat it by then." Ben was a notoriously slow eater, and everyone laughed at his promise.

"I'll tell you what, boys," broke in Dad, "I'll bet Mom doesn't feel much like smelling it cook, but if you'll take her into the living room and close the door, I'll make enough for all of us and bring it in a few minutes. Sarah, you get some glasses of water, and Janet, you get some bowls and napkins."

As Mom, Ben, and Jeff departed for the living room, Dad called after them. "And make her put her feet up, boys!" All of them laughed as Mom answered meekly, "Yes, sir!"

Chapter Six

*S*oon after Thanksgiving, there was a cold snap. For several days, snow fell from leaden gray skies, covering the earth with a soft white blanket. The younger children were excited every morning, discovering how much deeper the snow was than the day before. When the snow finally ended, Ben measured the depth again, and found it to be nearly sixteen inches. Blue skies returned and although the weather was still cold, the wind had stopped, making it pleasant to be outdoors, as long as one was warmly dressed.

The younger children made snow men and snow angels, and pulled each other on sleds around the yard. Jeff took them sledding on the hill in the pasture, and Janet and Ben helped Steve, Rachel, and Becky make snow houses in the big drifts beside the driveway where the snowplow had pushed large piles of snow off the gravel drive.

Sarah and Jeff took long hikes through the woods on snowshoes, enjoying the small winter birds in the trees. All the trees were beautiful, but the boughs of the evergreens, bent with their heavy burdens of snow, were the loveliest of all. At times the boughs almost bowed to the ground, nearly touching the path ahead of Sarah as she walked. God seemed so close in this setting - almost as if He were sharing wonderful secrets with these humans that He so graciously loved.

Mom and Dad used the snowshoes for a walk

in the woods daily, too. Mom felt so much better in the fresh air, surrounded by the winter sights and sounds. She was determined to exercise as much as she was able, without pushing herself too hard. Dad kept a close eye on her, only allowing Mom to walk a reasonable amount each day. She napped every afternoon, and it did seem to Sarah that Mom tired even more easily than she had when she was expecting Becky. Since that had been several years ago, Sarah couldn't trust her memory. Was Mom really more tired, or was Sarah simply older and more observant of Mom's symptoms?

Cooking the meals really was fun, although some days it was also a challenge. Sarah had helped with the cooking for years, usually cooking one or two meals a week. Having the responsibility of cooking day after day was a real change, though. Sarah had a new appreciation for Mom's cooking, even though she had always enjoyed the wonderful meals Mom made. She suddenly realized that cooking took not only preparation of the food itself, but planning ahead to make sure you had everything on hand and that the menu was varied.

Dad tried to give Sarah a break one night by bringing home some hamburgers and french fries from a nearby fast-food restaurant. The meal was welcomed by all, for food brought from a restaurant was a rare treat at the McLean house. However, being such a rare occurrence, most members of the family found themselves with slightly upset stomachs later that evening from the fried food. Poor Mom was unable to keep her meal down, and Sarah was reminded once again that sweet babies brought many kinds of sacri-

41

fice. When Dad checked on Mom a few minutes later, she just smiled weakly and assured him, "It's always worth it, David, when you hold them in your arms!"

Early January brought bitterly cold weather to southern Michigan, and everyone was cooped up indoors for a week. Jeff and Dad did all the chores, because Steve and Ben both had bad chest colds and Mom was hesitant to let them out in the wind, even just going to the barn and back. After the first few days, Ben seemed better, but Steve was coughing so hard on his ninth birthday that he couldn't really enjoy his cake. Mom finally put him to bed for a couple of days, hoping he would get better with rest.

"He just goes too hard," she confided to Sarah that evening. "He always has. I think that's why illness always hits him so hard. He doesn't give his body a chance to fight it. Steve insists he doesn't feel that bad, but I found him twice today on the living room floor, just lying there. That certainly isn't like Steve!"

During the night Sarah heard Mom get up several times and go into the boys' room. She knew Mom was checking on Steve and prayed for Steve's recovery and Mom's strength each time she woke up. When Mom came down in the morning, she looked tired and concerned. Steve's temperature had shot up suddenly during the night and Mom told Dad quietly, "I really feel that the Lord was telling me last night that Steve is very sick. Even with cough medicine, he can't stop coughing. He hardly slept at all last night. His fever is so high, I think he probably has pneumonia." Mom was really worried. "I gave the boys herbal teas and made sure they were warmly dressed, but I'm such a beginner at home remedies. I had just hoped we could hold off anything serious. I really don't like giving them medicine if it can be avoided."

"Kate," Dad replied, "just keep in mind that God can give doctors wisdom, too. Dr. Frank is a committed Christian and a very conservative doctor as well. You know he never prescribes anything unless he really feels it is necessary. Remember that God is Sovereign and He knows how sick Steve is. He is the One who must heal Steve, and He may choose to use doctors and medicines."

"You're right, David," Mom answered. "I'll just pray that God will give both you and Dr. Frank wisdom."

"Call Dr. Frank's office as soon as it opens at eight," Dad added. "See how quickly we can get Steve in. I think you should stay home and sleep this morning, since you didn't sleep much last night either. I'll take Steve in to the doctor and Sarah can handle everything here." Dad gave Mom a quick hug. "And don't worry, Kate. I'm sure Steve will be fine as soon as he gets some penicillin, if he really has pneumonia."

Mom smiled at Dad and nodded her head, but Sarah could see that she was still concerned. Dark shadows were under her eyes from lack of sleep, and Sarah wondered if Mom would even be able to sleep while Dad took Steve to the doctor.

Sure enough, Steve had pneumonia, and by lunchtime Dad was home with both Steve and the antibiotic. Mom felt much better after sleeping most of the morning, and tucked Steve right back into bed as soon as they came home. Dr. Frank had sent some cough medicine with codeine in it to help Steve stop coughing and he was able to sleep several hours the afternoon.

Jeff spent many hours with his younger brother in the next few days, reading to Steve and thinking up quiet activities for him to do in bed. "You're going to make a great father someday, Jeff," Mom told him appreciatively. "And Steve will remember your kindness for many years to come."

Jeff smiled at Mom. "I've had a good example you know," he reminded her. "Remember when I was a little guy, with that terrible case of chicken pox? Dad was always coming up with something to help take my mind off how miserable I felt. I'll remember that for years to come, too."

After a few days, Steve was up and around again and, except for a lingering cough, he seemed almost back to his old self. Mom, Dad, Sarah, and Jeff were constantly having to remind him to slow down, or his cough might worsen again. The weather was still very cold, and now Sarah and Janet found themselves stretched to the limits of their patience, trying to find activities to keep the younger children busy and contented indoors.

Sarah prayed for wisdom and strength, and found that God always answered. Many times ideas would suddenly pop into her head, or she would be inspired to sing with the younger ones as she let them help her with the work. Every few days, it was nice enough for Janet to take the little girls out for a while. Steve, however, had to wait two weeks before he was well enough to go outside with a muffler tied around his face.

Some days Sarah wondered where Mom found the strength to keep as cheerful as she did, with all the nausea and fatigue added to the younger children's pent-up energy needing an outlet. Sarah found herself slowly becoming discouraged as the weeks wore on. Would the winter never end?

One cold day in February, Dad handed Sarah a letter that had come in the mail. Sarah uttered an exclamation of surprise as she glanced at the return address. The letter was from a pen pal, Hannah. Sarah hadn't heard from Hannah in months and had been so busy herself that she had not even wondered once why Hannah had not written. Putting the envelope in her pocket, Sarah waited until the little girls had finished helping her with the dishes. After getting them settled with some homemade Playdough at the kitchen table, she went upstairs to the girls' room to enjoy the letter in a few moments of peace and quiet.

As she eagerly tore open the envelope and began reading the letter, sudden tears smarted her eyes. Hannah's letter told Sarah that she was nearing the end of a wonderful courtship and planned to be married in early April. "I'm sorry I haven't written in so long, but I have been truly busier than I have ever been before," Hannah's letter ended. "I also wanted to wait and see if God was leading John and I to marry before I wrote you. We both feel sure now that He has brought us together, and all of our parents agree. What a happy time this is for me! My highest hopes are being fulfilled. Please pray for us as we make plans and continue to grow closer to each other. Your sister in Christ, Hannah."

Sarah slowly folded the letter and pulled a Kleenex out of her pocket. She was thankful she had waited to read the letter until she had a few quiet moments alone. She truly was happy that Hannah was going to be married and glad that she and John had built their relationship on courtship rather than dating. But Sarah had to admit to herself that she was also envious. Why wasn't she being courted? Why did she have to wait, while Hannah was preparing for marriage?

Chapter Seven

Sarah heard Mom quietly get up from her afternoon rest and start down the steps. "Mom?" Sarah called softly. "Mom, can you come in here?"

Mom's footsteps returned from the landing and she came to the door of Sarah's room. "Why Sarah, what are you doing up here? You look like you've been crying. Are you all right sweetheart?" Mom asked in surprise.

"Oh Mom," Sarah began. She had thought she was through crying, but at Mom's loving concern she began crying all over again. "Hannah is getting married and I'm so afraid I never will."

Mom's arms went around Sarah, and Sarah cried on Mom's shoulder as though she was Becky's age again. Mom hugged her close, and patted her back, waiting for her to calm down a little before she spoke. Finally, Sarah gave Mom a tight squeeze, then sat up and blew her nose.

"I'm sorry, Mom. I didn't mean to cry so hard. I thought I was doing better, but it seems that I trust God about the future for a while and then I go through a struggle all over again. Maybe I just want to get married too much, but sometimes it seems like I'll never be completely happy until God gives me a husband and children. Is that wrong, Mom? What can I do? How can I wait patiently for Him to show me His will?"

Mom was silent for a moment. Then she reached for Sarah's hand, closed her eyes, and began praying aloud softly. "Heavenly Father, please give me the wisdom I need to answer Sarah's questions. Help me to point her to Jesus. Help us both to trust You for our futures, knowing You love us and that You promise to work all things for our good. In Jesus' name. Amen."

Opening her eyes, she smiled at Sarah. "Sarah," Mom began, "you certainly are my daughter. If there ever was a girl who longed to get married and have a house full of children, I was that girl and now you have that same longing. I believe that God Himself is the one Who put the desire to be a wife and mother in your heart. Having the desire to be married is not sinful at all. Proverbs 18:22 says, 'Whoso findeth a wife findeth a good thing, and obtaineth favor of the Lord.' But Sarah, if that desire is put above our desire to have God's will for our lives, then it is not pleasing to Him. Yes, your wish for marriage is a very difficult thing to give over to Him. There are many situations in my own life where it has been difficult to say, 'Thy will be done.' I have struggled many times over desires, just as you have, first trusting God, then doubting that I could let go of my own wants. I think most Christians would tell you that they have had the same experience."

Mom paused thoughtfully, then said, "You know Sarah, Jesus was tempted as we are and yet He prayed in the garden of Gethsemane, 'Not my will, but Thine be done.' And we have Him as our advocate to the Father. If we call on Him, He will not turn us away. We must call on Him, though. Daily. Hourly. Whenever we are tempted to dwell on ourselves and what we want. We must believe that He truly is all wise and all good and all holy, and He will give us what is best. We must call on Him when we are afraid or doubting."

Mom looked at Sarah. "You are still very young, Sarah. You won't be 20 for several months yet. God may bring a husband to you soon, a few years from now, many years from now, or never. But trusting God and learning to wait on Him to reveal His will to you won't end as long as you live here on earth, whether you marry or not. Don't let yourself dwell on marriage and courtship. Trust God and let Him do everything in His own time."

"It's just hard sometimes," Sarah slowly admitted.

"I know, Sarah," said Mom. "But God has promised to conform us to the image of His Son, and this is part of that process. I'll pray for you Sarah, and you can also pray for me, as well as for all the other Christians you know, that we will desire His will above our own. Maybe God would have you especially pray for other young women going through the same struggles you are, even those you've never met."

"Oh Mom, what a good idea!" Sarah exclaimed. "I think that will really help me - even just remembering that there are other girls who are going through the same thing somehow makes me feel better."

"And Sarah," Mom added, "perhaps there is a girl somewhere right now praying for you, too, even though she doesn't know you." Mom gave Sarah a quick hug. Suddenly, the sound of dishes and pans crashing to the floor was heard all over the house. Mom stood up and said, "I'd better go and see what that was! Come on down when you're ready."

"Thanks, Mom. I'll be there soon. And Mom," Sarah shyly hesitated before she finished her sentence, "I sure am glad God gave me Christian parents who love me so much. I hope if it is His will for me to marry and have children, that He will someday let me be as good a mother as you are."

"If I am a good mother, it is only by God's grace, not my own goodness. I love you, Sarah." With that, Mom left to go downstairs and Sarah dropped on her knees beside her bed, pouring out her calmer heart to God in prayer.

Chapter Eight

$\mathcal{T}$im had been waiting a long time to again ask Sarah out for a date. It wasn't that he wasn't interested anymore. It was just that the situation never presented itself. Oh, she had come to the market a number of times since his last, painful encounter with her. But she always had her sister, mother or brother with her. No matter how much he wanted to date Sarah, he just was not going to talk to her about it with her family hanging around listening.

Sarah sure seemed different from all the other girls that he had known. For one thing, she looked different. She never wore clothes that looked like she was trying to attract attention to herself. She seemed to always wear some kind of a skirt or dress that was sort of long. Come to think of it, her clothes seemed to match her personality. Shy? No, not really. She was friendly enough to other shoppers who spoke to her or smiled at her. Just kind of quiet and reserved though.

And although she never seemed in a big hurry, Tim had noticed that Sarah always chose her purchases quickly and didn't linger at the market. It was as though she had better things to do or something more interesting waiting for her. Maybe that was why she seemed so different –so much more mature than the loud, silly girls who often came to the market, trying to be noticed. Even George referred to her as a "young lady," though it may have been unconscious on his part. Tim had never even heard George use the term "young lady" before. He always just called them "girls."

Anyway, Tim reflected, Sarah was different. And hard to get to know. Would he ever get the chance to date her?

Tim had thought about that last encounter many, many times over the last months. How had she phrased it? Wasn't it "Thanks, Tim, but it's not possible."? So what were the reasons it was "not possible"? He could only think of three reasons. First, maybe she was dating someone else and didn't want to break it off with the other guy. That didn't seem likely, though, because Tim had never seen her with another guy, except for her family members. Besides, if that were the case she would have probably told him outright, like, "I'm sorry, but I'm dating this guy named Ned right now." Second, maybe it was because she didn't like him and was trying to brush him off. But if that was the case, she would have said something a little more sarcastic, like, "Thanks but no thanks!" He had sure heard that a few times from other girls he had tried to date. No, her answer was much too kind and polite to indicate that she didn't like him at all. Third, maybe it was because she already had something planned for that weekend. Yeah, that had to be it! That was certainly understandable. All he had to do was find a weekend that she was free and ask her for a date then. He waited for that opportunity.

It was a snowy Wednesday afternoon in late February when Sarah walked into the market alone.

She was trying to brush some of the snow off her clothes as Tim moved in her direction. "Okay, here goes!" he thought. "It's now or never!"

"Did you ever see so much snow?" he asked, walking up close to Sarah. "I think we should start thinking about building igloos or something." That wasn't the brightest comment he could have made, he reflected, but he felt tremendous pressure to get the ball rolling fast and it was the first thing that came into his mind.

"Yes, it sure is snowing hard," Sarah replied. Although Tim seemed a little nervous about this encounter, Sarah certainly felt no fear in talking to him. She knew she had already told him that she would not date him. She was sure that this friendly chit-chat would stay just that.

"I imagine Jeff is working hard these days, huh?" Tim stated, reflecting back on his conversation with Jeff and her several months earlier. Sarah did not remember all the details of that conversation, however, and simply replied, "Yes, I suppose he is."

"Say, Sarah, I know you're probably busy and need to get home with some groceries." He paused, then continued, "I have two tickets to the basketball game this weekend. They're really good tickets, too. They're mid-court, only about 15 rows up! Tickets like that don't come along every day, do they? Think you would like to go with me? I could pick you up at around 4:00 on Saturday. That way we could get something to eat first. I know this really neat restaurant that serves Chinese. What do you say?"

All in all, Tim was pleased with the way he

pulled it off. He felt he had asked for a date in a nice way, had offered her a really fun place to go, and had thrown in a great meal to boot! Who could resist such an offer? Of course, it would set him back a few bucks, but what's money for if you can't spend it on someone you like?

Once again, Sarah was speechless. Didn't Tim get the message the last time? Why was he doing this to her? She just wanted to buy some carrots and lettuce. But now she had to confront this situation also.

Above all, Sarah wanted to be kind and clear. "I'm sorry, Tim. I must not have explained myself very clearly the last time we, ah, . . . talked."

"Sure, you said you couldn't go. Probably had something else planned. That's okay. How about this weekend, though? I know a lot of people who would die to see this game. What do you say?"

"I'm sorry. But I have chosen not to date, Tim. Not anyone . . . ," Sarah started, but Tim interrupted her.

"You're not going to date anyone? Are you going to be a nun?" Tim questioned, seeming genuinely embarrassed. "If so, I'm sorry! I know how important that kind of stuff is to a nun. My neighbor's aunt is a nun. She's real nice, but says she can never date or get married."

"No, Tim," said Sarah. "I'm not planning on being a nun. It's just that I have decided to engage in courtship instead of dating. That's all. You may not know much about courtship, and that's okay. But it's what I have chosen, and I'm very committed to following that path. So you see I can't accept your invitation for a date. Not your invitation, nor any other boy's invitation. You're very nice to understand."

But Tim didn't understand. And he said so. "If you're not going to date, how are you going to find someone to marry? I'm pretty confused." He had never heard of this thing called courtship. He had heard his grandparents talk about courting, but he knew that was just an old-fashioned way to say dating.

Sarah didn't think that the produce section of a market was the proper place to explain the concept of courtship to Tim. Nor did she think she was the one who should be instructing him in it. So, politely, she turned and said, "I'm really sorry, Tim. Courtship would take a long time to explain and I'm not sure I could do a very good job of it. If you really want to know more about it, I could try to find a man to explain it to you. I'm sorry but I'm going to have to get my shopping done right now. I have to have this produce for supper."

With that she turned and started to walk toward the carrots. She was glad the episode was over and hoped that Tim had not been offended. To her amazement, she heard Tim calling her.

"Sarah, I think you need to think this through real carefully. As you said, I don't know everything about this courtship business. I'm afraid, though, that it might cause you to miss out on meeting someone, . . . someone nice," Tim faltered. He didn't want to puff himself up, but he did think he was a pretty nice guy. Why couldn't she see that? "Besides, it doesn't sound like too much fun if you can't go out with a guy every now and then."

"I have lots of fun in life, Tim. Really I do. It's just that in that area of my life I have decided to follow what I feel God has planned for me," she answered.

Hearing the word "God" brought a new idea to Tim's head. "I know you are a religious person and all that, because I've seen you talking to the preacher a couple of times in here. I respect that. Honest I do. I know for a fact that many religious people do date. I've seen them! They look like they're having fun and everything. I've even seen them at basketball games. Won't you reconsider?"

"I'm sorry, Tim. I've given my answer and my reasons. I'll pray that God will help you understand. Please forgive me if anything I've said has hurt you. But the answer is, and must be, 'No'. Both now and in the future. I'm not going to date. Now, I'm sorry but I really have to get home with these things." Sarah moved away and picked up the first bunch of carrots and the first head of lettuce she saw. Moving quickly, she paid for her items and left the store.

"Sarah, please say 'Maybe' instead of 'Never.'" Tim had followed her out of the store!

Sarah was a little frightened. Was he going to follow her home? Would he start popping up whenever she took a walk or played in the yard with her brothers and sisters? The only thing she knew to do was pray. Silently, she prayed that God would help Tim see that her answer was final. And that God would protect her. Turning, she said, "I'm afraid I will never date, Tim. Good-bye."

As she walked further, she half-expected to hear

his footsteps racing toward hers. But the only thing she heard was the sound of a bird, singing beautifully somewhere close by. After a few more feet, she couldn't resist the urge and turned around to see if Tim was following her. He was standing, back about where he would have been when he had asked his final question. He was looking at her but didn't say anything more. How she prayed that he had finally understood! Home had never looked so good to her as it did that day when she finally reached it. Home was a place of protection, a place where she felt loved and understood!

"Hey Sarah," Jeff called from the side of the house, where he was stacking wood with Dad. "I was beginning to worry about you. It took a long time just to pick up a few items. Did you have any trouble?"

"Thank you God, for brothers!" Sarah prayed silently. Then she answered, "No, I'm fine. I better get this in the house, though, so we can eat soon. I've got to start supper right away." With that she turned and walked into the house.

Chapter Nine

"I'm thankful today is Sunday," Sarah thought to herself. She needed a day of rest after all the busyness of this past week. It was a week of one catastrophe after another! On Monday, Becky had burned her hand badly on the stove and needed lots of love and attention from everyone. Tuesday, Steve fell out of a tree and, although he didn't break any bones, he had been sick for a few days. His smile was noticeably missing. Mom and Dad were afraid he might have suffered a concussion, but he seemed to be okay now. On Thursday, Jeff was using the chain saw as he had done for over a year. Jeff was known in his family as the "safety nut," and always tried to be as safe and careful as possible. Yet on that day, the saw had suddenly kicked back for no apparent reason, knocking him to the ground and spraining his wrist badly. Then, just yesterday, Sarah herself had fallen down the last few steps while carrying a load of laundry to the basement. She, too, was spared any serious injury. Yet she experienced extreme pain for several hours and her leg became quite swollen and bruised. Yes, she needed this day of rest.

The McLeans arrived at the meeting house about ten minutes before the service was to begin and sat down. Sarah took this opportunity to pray silently and reflect on the goodness of God. Yes, it had been a week of catastrophes, yet no one was seriously hurt. In fact, God's angels had been guarding them from serious injury, it seemed to Sarah.

As she finished her prayer, she raised her head and looked over the other people who had come to worship. It was always assuring and comforting to see so many of the same families in church each Sunday. There were the Yoders. Both Mr. and Mrs. Yoder were now over 90 years old and yet they had a love for God which strengthened and encouraged everyone in the church. Their children and grandchildren now attended this same church too. What a blessing that must have been to Mr. and Mrs. Yoder, to be reminded of the mercies of God in such a visible way each Sunday.

Over there were the Aslingers. How the church had prayed when Mrs. Aslinger had been diagnosed with cancer! God had chosen to bless Mrs. Aslinger with a remission of the cancer, at least for the time being. All of the prayer and meals prepared for the Aslingers had brought the church closer together. Mrs. Aslinger had a mature spirit about the whole thing and just prayed that God's will for her life would be done. Such a strengthening example!

And on the other side were the Baileys. Mr. and Mrs. Bailey had seven children, whose ages were close to those of her own family. In fact, the two families were quite good friends with each other. "It's too bad they don't have a girl about my age, though," Sarah thought and sighed a little. "If they did, I could talk about my hopes and fears and she could do the same." As it was, she relied on pen pals for encouragement about courtship.

As her head turned back toward the front, her eyes caught sight of a new family that she didn't remember ever seeing in church before. It looked to her like a father with his four children, two boys and two girls. One boy was about Sarah's age while the other looked to be around fifteen. The girls seemed to be a lot younger, maybe eight and 10. "I wonder where the mother is?" Sarah thought. Before she could entertain any other thoughts, however, she quickly turned her head. The preacher had called the congregation to bow their heads in prayer in preparation for the church service to begin.

The pastor's sermon was strong and direct as usual. His message could have been titled "Telling the Truth." He started off with a quotation from a famous American. "A well-known poet once made this statement, 'Sell your horses before they die. The secret to success in life is passing along your losses to other people.' Let that sink in a minute. Let me repeat it for you. 'Sell your horses before they die. The secret to success in life is passing along your losses to other people.'

"Does that statement reflect God's will for His followers? What if we as Christians operated with that philosophy central to our being? Would we be stronger Christians or weaker ones? Let's take a look at what God's Word tells us."

The preacher then read a number of passages from the Scriptures. He expounded upon Leviticus 19:11, Colossians 3:8-11, and I Timothy 1:8-11 in which God commanded His people not to lie or to deceive others. He then read the sobering verses found in Psalm 116:5-11 which proclaimed that all men were liars. "Who is our grand example for lying?" he asked the congregation. "Is it Jesus? NO. Then who is it? John 8:42-44 will shed some light on this." The pastor turned in his Bible and revealed that Satan is the father of lies, and is sometimes referred to as "The Great Deceiver."

Having shown that lying is not God's will for His believers, the preacher then moved to several practical applications. "First," he stated, "do not lie. Do not make a statement that you know is false." He followed this by giving several examples of times he had heard Christians lie in order to save money or protect their reputation.

"Second," he continued, "do not even subtly deceive. By that I mean do not deliberately misrepresent the facts by words or actions in order to further your own interests. Let me give you an example. Let's say you are going to sell a horse. Now, unfortunately you know that the horse tends to go lame easily if you ride it too much in a day. Suppose you get tired of this condition, and decide to sell the horse. To your joy a potential buyer comes by to look at it. Fortunately, the horse is not limping today, probably because you purposefully haven't ridden it for several days just to make sure he doesn't go lame right when a buyer shows up. The buyer looks over the horse carefully and says, 'That's a fine looking animal you have there. It sure looks healthy to me!' If you fail to volunteer the fact that the horse goes lame easily, you are deceiving the buyer! Now, that may take some of you by surprise. After all 'Buyer Beware' is the rule of business, isn't it? But what else could you call it, when you examine the situation? Why else would you not tell the buyer about the horse's condition, except that you are afraid it might make you lose the sale or get less money for the horse? It's deception! And it happens all the time. Oh God, forgive us as your chosen people for engaging in such activities!" he prayed aloud. The preacher then related other examples of subtly deceiving someone else.

Then, speaking softly, almost as though his next words were a dream of his, he continued, "What if buying something from a Christian was different from buying something from someone else? What if it was common knowledge that if you bought anything from a Christian you were going to be told everything about the item, both good and bad points? What if the world knew that if they bought anything from a Christian that they would get a fair and square deal? Wouldn't that make us stand out? Wouldn't that be a positive example to the world? Wouldn't that make us the salt of the earth? Sadly, though, that is not the case today. May God make it so, especially for those of us gathered here today!"

"Third," the pastor continued with practical applications, "do not make others engage in deceit on your behalf. That is, don't make others lie for you. How could you do that? Oh, it's easy actually. For example, the father might have instructed his son not to mention to the horse buyer about the horse's lame condition. When we do this kind of thing, not only are we sinning, but we are also forcing someone else to sin."

After providing several other applications and examples, the preacher concluded, "We, as Christians who have been redeemed by the blood of the Lamb, are to be different from the world! The book of Matthew reflects this in several places, where Jesus instructed us to be pure in heart, to be the salt of the earth, and to be the light of the world. Oh, may He help us follow His will in this matter, starting today." The pastor prayed that God would cause the members of His church to live their lives in accordance with His will, and not to just reflect the ways of the world.

As Sarah traveled home, she contemplated what the preacher had said. She had always thought of herself as an honest girl. But how many times she had been guilty of subtly deceiving another? It was what she didn't say in those instances that was so sinful. She prayed that God would forgive her and help her to be honest and not even subtly deceive others.

"They're the Locke family," she heard Dad saying to Mom as Sarah finished this prayer. "They just moved here from another area. The father, John, seemed like a nice man. He served as an elder in the congregation they moved from. It's sad though. I learned from Nels, who had met and talked to John Locke this week, that Mrs. Locke died about seven years ago. He's had a pretty tough time trying to farm and still raise those four children these last seven years."

"Why don't we have them out to the house?" Mom asked. "We could ask them to dinner this weekend and let his children get to know our children. Oh, how hard that would be to raise a family alone!"

"I'm not sure you need to push yourself and

make a big meal," Dad answered, with concern in his voice. "Are you sure you feel up to it?"

"With Sarah's and Janet's help and everyone else pitching in extra hard, I doubt if I would have to do anything harder than normal. I'll bet they would like a good home-cooked meal about now. I can imagine how hard it must be to get meals prepared just when you are moving in. Besides, they don't have any big girls to do the cooking like I do."

"Well, okay," Dad said, "if everyone promises to pitch in and help. What do you say gang?" Most everyone had tuned into Mom and Dad's conversation and all agreed heartily. All of them wished to make it an expression of hospitality.

"Okay, I'll go by and extend the invitation this afternoon then," Dad replied.

Chapter Ten

"They're here! They're here!" Becky cried with delight, looking out the window late Friday afternoon.

"Really?" exclaimed Rachel in excitement. "Can I open the door to let them in, Mommy? Please?"

"You certainly may, Rachel," smiled Mom. "And Steve, you may show them where to put their coats and gloves."

"Hello folks!" greeted Dad as the Locke family came into the house. "We're glad you could come."

"Thanks for having us," returned John Locke. "You were kind to invite us." Turning to his children, Mr. Locke introduced them. "This is James," Mr. Locke began. "He is my oldest son, and farms with me. James is twenty years old, and a good, dependable worker. Michael is fifteen, and also helps quite a bit on the farm, besides being our fix-it man. Ruth is eleven, and Naomi is nine. They do a fine job helping around the house. And I promise not to ask your age, David, if you won't ask mine," he ended with a laugh.

Dad chuckled, "It's a deal, John." Then he proceeded to introduce Mom and the children. When he had finished, Mom added, "Steve would like to show you where to hang your coats, and then I think we'll be ready to eat."

After the blessing, Dad asked Mr. Locke where

they had lived before moving to the community.

"We lived about 50 miles north of here," Mr. Locke replied. "The soil isn't as good as it is in this area, and when James decided two years ago to go into partnership with me, we began to look around a bit. We decided on this area because the land was pretty close in price to our old place, and it is only about twenty miles away from the children's grandparents. Our neighbor's son and his wife really wanted to buy our farm, to make it easier for the son to work with his father. Everything worked out well for all of us and we decided to move during late winter. That way we could be well settled and ready to plant as soon as spring comes."

During supper the McLean and Locke families got to know each other better and all of them greatly enjoyed the meal and fellowship. Sarah was especially interested to hear Mr. Locke mention that he and his wife had become interested in the idea of courtship for their children the year before Mrs. Locke died. "Since that time I have become completely convinced that courtship is what God wants for my family. And I am very thankful that my children are in agreement with me," Mr. Locke told the McLeans. "As a matter of fact, that is one of the things that drew me to your church. I had been told that there were several families in your fellowship who were also planning on courtship for their children. Of course, that isn't the most important thing in choosing a group to worship with, but I felt that our beliefs would probably agree in most other areas, too. And so far, they have," he added with a smile.

"Yes, there are several families who are committed to courtship in our church," Dad assured their visitors. "Most of them have younger children, but we are glad that they have made the decision early. We haven't had anyone in the church who has actually gone through a full courtship yet, but our family and the Eaton family both have children approaching the right ages." Sarah felt herself blush at that last comment. Dad continued, "Perhaps some will walk that path soon, so that the younger ones will be encouraged to follow."

After supper, Sarah, Janet, and Mom cleaned up the kitchen while Dad and Mr. McLean went to the living room to sit by the fire. Jeff, Ben, and Steve took James and Michael with them to the barn to look over the animals, while Ruth and Naomi sweetly offered to read books to Rachel and Becky.

"Yes, the last seven years have been hard, as you can imagine, David," Mr. Locke replied to a query from Dad. "Linda, that was my wife's name, and I had a very close, loving marriage. She was my best friend, too." Here, he paused for a few minutes. Dad didn't speak, knowing that Mr. Locke was reliving some past experiences in his mind. As he continued, he had a calm look on his face. "Yes, it's been hard. But you know, I have to admit to you that it has also been a time of real spiritual growth for me. I have come to know the Lord and His will for my life in a new way in the last seven years."

John continued, "God has strengthened and encouraged me so wonderfully. He has taught me that He can supply all of my needs! I'm sorry to say that while Linda was alive, I felt like I had to have her or I just couldn't live. When we found out she had cancer and only had a few months to live, I almost fell apart. How could I live without her? Well, like I said, God has taught me that I can not only live, but actually enjoy life too. Do I still miss her?" he paused, his eyes misting over. "Do I miss her? Yes, oh yes," he said with deep feeling. "But God has helped me find my joy in Him."

Dad was quiet, almost reverent for a few minutes. To hear such a testimony of God's power was both uplifting and a little sobering to David McLean. Dad prayed that he would have John's strength if anything ever happened to Mom.

"That's a wonderful testimony, John," Dad quietly stated.

"Oh, I don't want you to get the wrong idea," John humbly replied. "It's not because of me or anything I have done. No, it's all because of the power of God. May He get all the glory and honor!"

Dad and Mr. Locke continued talking for some time, sharing what the Lord had taught them and the challenges He had helped them weather. Sharing with a new Christian friend is such a blessing. Dad was very impressed with Mr. Locke's humility, love for his family, and love for his Lord.

A little while later the Locke family thanked the McLeans again for their hospitality and left for their own home. As soon as the door had closed, Dad turned to his family and remarked, "The Lockes certainly seem to be a nice family. How are you feeling, Kate? Did it tire you too much to have company?"

"Oh no," Mom replied. "I feel fine. Sarah and Janet hardly let me help much with the dishes. I just enjoyed watching my sweet daughters do my work! It really is a blessing to have a large family. I feel very well cared for," Mom added, looking around at them all. "No woman could ask for more."

"The Lockes are so nice!" Janet jumped in. "I just think they are one of the nicest families we have ever met. When can we have them over again? Can it be soon?"

Dad laughed and shook his head. "Janet, they just left. They're not even home yet! Let's wait a little while, okay?"

After evening family devotions, Mom took the younger ones up for a bedtime story as usual. "Mommy," began Steve as he climbed into his bed, "What's a pest?"

"A pest?" Mom asked in surprise. "A pest is usually a bothersome insect, like a fly or mosquito. What made you think of pests in March?"

"Well," Steve said slowly, "you know the biggest boy here tonight, James? He said something about little boys being pests, when we were out at the barn. What did he mean Mommy? Was he talking about me and Ben? He didn't seem very happy about us going along with the big boys."

Mom hesitated, then answered Steve slowly, "I don't really know, son. I hope not. Don't worry about it. At our house we are all glad to have little boys around."

"But Jeff is always glad to have us to go with him, no matter where he goes. Why wasn't James glad too?" persisted Steve.

"Maybe since he has no little brothers, he doesn't know how wonderful it is to have them," answered Mom. "And sometimes people repeat things they have heard others say, without thinking of whether or not they are kind. Let's not think that James really meant to be unkind. Let's get to know him better, and then perhaps he'll see how nice it is to have little boys around."

"Okay Mommy," Steve agreed cheerfully. He settled down quickly to listen to the story, as if he had already forgotten all about the incident.

Later, Mom mentioned to Dad what Steve had told her about James' comment. "Hmm," mused Dad. "That's strange. I was just going to tell you how impressed I was with John Locke and his faith. He seems like such a mature Christian. Of course, even if James said something like that, it doesn't change who John is. And perhaps Steve was mistaken. We need to remember not to judge James. Let's try to forget it and just see what happens in the future. Unruffle your feathers, mother hen," he added, smiling. "It really isn't that big of a problem."

"Oh, of course not, David," Mom agreed. "I just tend to get my feathers ruffled pretty easily, I'm afraid. Tell me more about what John said."

Chapter Eleven

*D*uring the next two months, the McLean and Locke families saw each other several times. At church, they usually talked for a short while after the sermon was over. The McLean family was able to introduce the Lockes to several other Christian families in the community, some of whom attended other churches in the area. On Easter, the Locke family was invited to the McLean home and the families enjoyed having dinner together again, remembering the Resurrection. In April, James spent all of one day helping Jeff replace a part on his tractor, and joined Sarah's family for lunch that day. The following day he returned, without being asked, to help Jeff repair some fence in an older part of the pasture that had not been used for some years. Jeff had spoken to James the day before about his hopes to re-open that section as the McLean's growing herd of beef cattle could use the extra grazing area this summer. But no one, including Jeff, had dreamed that a cheerful James would show up at eight o'clock the next morning in work clothes and heavy gloves.

"Ready to tackle that fence, Jeff?" he grinned as Jeff answered the door. His help was much appreciated and everyone agreed that John Locke was certainly right when he described James as hard working and dependable.

Mom was feeling fine now, and Sarah was only

too glad to let her take over the main part of the cooking again. She continued to cook twice a week, though, or any time that Mom seemed especially tired. Sarah used these cooking days to teach Janet more cooking and baking skills, although Janet was able to cook several things on her own. She and Janet also alternated with the laundry and dishes, letting the little girls continue to be their helpers. Mom was able to get some sewing done that she had been hoping to finish before summer, so the household ran very smoothly that spring.

Seeds had been ordered in February, and Sarah and Janet planned to be in charge of the garden this year, with only advice and direction from Mom. Ben, Steve, Rachel, and Becky promised to help with hoeing and weeding and, as Sarah said, "If six of us can't handle the garden this year, there is no reason but laziness!"

As the weather warmed again and spring returned in earnest, May 5th came and Sarah celebrated her 20th birthday. It seemed like a milestone somehow to her, and she seemed to hear a refrain in her mind - "You're twenty now and no courtship yet."

Sarah tried to keep too busy to let her mind wander. She knew it was important to keep her thoughts on the Lord, her family, and her work. Mom had admonished her not to dwell on courtship. But especially at quiet times of day, when she sat embroidering or knitting in the evenings, or just before she drifted off to sleep, she found her mind again wandering to thoughts of courtship, marriage, and a home and family of her own.

She truly did make an effort to put it out of her mind each time, to not dwell on courtship or the future as Mom had wisely advised her. Nevertheless, if her mind was not fully occupied, she found her thoughts drifting again. And she had to admit to herself that those thoughts often turned to James Locke.

Was he the man God would lead to her? His family and background were similar in many ways to hers, as were his interests. With Jeff, Sarah shared an interest in animals, gardening, and farm life. She knew she could share the same things with James, who was already a full-time farmer. He was polite and respectful to her parents as well as to Sarah herself. He certainly seemed to enjoy his friendship with Jeff, which pleased Sarah since she was so close to this special brother. And James truly was a dependable, hard worker. He seemed to get along really well with his father and did his share of their work gladly.

At that point, Sarah's thoughts always started becoming tangled. Why was it that she wasn't completely sure that James would be right for her? Was it just a defense mechanism because he hadn't expressed an interest in her yet? She knew James was a Christian. He was even committed to courtship. At least she would never have to face an uncomfortable encounter with him, the way she had to at the market with Tim twice before!

As the months went by, Sarah continued to try to keep her mind on anything and everything besides courtship and James. She made sure that her behavior around him was above reproach, always greeting him in a friendly way at church or when he came to the house to ask for Jeff, but never lingering long to talk with him. She prayed frequently that God would help her to wait patiently for Him to reveal His will. Sarah also frequently reminded herself that James was primarily Jeff's friend, although that was clear anyway.

James obviously enjoyed the company of Jeff and Dad and he was always quite friendly and polite with Mom, Sarah, and Janet. In fact, he was also polite to the younger children, but she couldn't really say he was friendly to them. Thinking back, Sarah remembered one cold and windy day in April, the day after Rachel's sixth birthday. James came to the house, and Rachel, still excited from the day before, greeted James joyfully as she opened the door. Sarah was in the kitchen starting lunch and overheard Rachel chattering about the small toy cradle she had received for her dolls. James merely said, "Um hmm, that's nice. Is Jeff busy this morning?" Sarah wondered why that should bother her so. James wasn't rude, or rough, or even unkind to Rachel. He was just so . . . well, maybe "distant" was the word. Disinterested. Completely disinterested. Sarah supposed that six-year-old girls and doll cradles weren't really very interesting to a young man, but the incident still disturbed her somehow.

Perhaps she was expecting too much. After all, James was grown-up and had no really young brothers and sisters, although Ruth and Naomi were close to the ages of Ben and Steve. They didn't seem to have a really close relationship with James, but then, she hardly ever saw them together anyway. The Locke sisters were always reading books to the younger

McLean girls or helping them play house when the families were together.

At other times, James came to the house alone or with Michael to work with Jeff and Dad. Sarah didn't know much about what went on at the Locke house. Jeff rarely mentioned much beyond the work he had helped with when he had gone to the Locke place and Sarah didn't like to ask him.

Chapter Twelve

One evening in late May, Mom and Sarah sat at the kitchen table, patterns and fabric piled in stacks around them. They were trying to decide what dresses and jumpers the little girls would need for the fall. Mom hoped to get as much as possible of the fall sewing done before the baby was born. Since the baby was due in August, that didn't leave many weeks. "But I'm sure we can do it," Mom assured Sarah, as well as herself. "After all, we have almost everything finished that you and Janet and I will need, and Janet will be a big help. She has really done well with the last few things she has made. Perhaps I'll let her make the girls' winter nightgowns. That will be plenty for her to do, since the weeds seem to be keeping all of you busy in the garden. It has been so long since I really looked over the garden. How are the herbs doing?"

Sarah was just about to reply when the front screen door banged shut. "That must be Jeff, back from the Lockes," Sarah said. "I'll bet he's tired. It's after seven and he left at seven this morning. Hi, Jeff," she smiled as he walked into the kitchen. "Can I get you some cold lemonade?"

"That really sounds good. Thanks!" Jeff slumped into Dad's chair at the head of the table and sighed. Then he looked out of the window beside the kitchen cupboard in thoughtful silence. Sarah poured

the lemonade and set it beside him, but Jeff didn't seem
aware of her, Mom, or the lemonade.

Mom and Sarah exchanged concerned glances.
This just wasn't like Jeff at all. Softly Mom asked, "Is
anything wrong, Jeff?"

Jeff slowly brought his gaze back to the table
and shrugged his shoulders. "I don't know. Not really,
I guess. I . . . oh, I don't know. I like James pretty
well, and Mr. Locke sure is a fine Christian man,
but . . ." his voice trailed off. Sighing, he began again.
"James is just somehow different from me, I guess.
Ruth and Naomi made lunch for us today, and they
really did a good job for such young girls. Mr. Locke
and Michael and I all told them we appreciated the
meal. Even though the corn was scorched and biscuits
were hard, we could honestly tell them that the chicken
and potatoes were great. You could tell they felt anxious about the meal and had tried hard to please 'the
men.'"

Here Jeff grew silent again momentarily, then
slowly he added, "But James ignored them through
the whole meal. He just sort of acted like they weren't
there. It's hard to describe, really. It wasn't like he
deliberately ignored them and he certainly wasn't rude
or unkind. It was just as though he hardly realized
they even existed. The girls didn't seem hurt about it
though. Maybe they're used to it, I don't know. That's
pretty typical of how it goes every time I am around
there. None of my business, really. Like I said, he
wasn't unkind to them. When he got up to go back
outside he did say, 'Thanks, girls,' and smiled at them.
But that's the extent of the attention he gives them

ever, at least when I'm around.

"With Dad and me, he always goes out of his way to be friendly and interested in everything we say and do. Maybe he just has problems relating to younger kids. It's certainly not a fatal flaw in his personality. It's just hard for me to understand, that's all. I really love children. They seem to add so much to life for me. I'm glad I'm not a mom or even going to be one someday. I'm not cut out for some of that stuff! But James is really missing out on a wonderful part of life, to just isolate himself in an adult world as much as possible. At least, that seems to me what he is doing. Maybe not. Maybe I'm just tired."

Jeff smiled apologetically. "Sorry to go on for so long. It sure is good to have some listening ears. But I really am beat! I think I'll go on up to bed and read awhile. James lent me this biography of Hudson Taylor and I'll try to start it, if I don't fall asleep. Good night ladies," he finished.

Sarah and her mother watched as Jeff went around the corner to go up the steps. "Whoa!" they heard him exclaim. "Where did you come from? I didn't know I had another pair of listening ears! I expect that Mom would be interested in seeing you, Janet." He continued up the stairs to the boys' room.

"I certainly would!" Mom exclaimed. "Janet, what are you doing? I sent you to find the little girls and start their baths. Why are you on the steps, listening to other people's conversations?"

A red-faced, but undaunted, Janet came into the kitchen to face Mom. "I did go to find the girls, but they weren't upstairs. Then I got their nightclothes out for them and was coming down. I just sat on the steps to rest for a minute," she finished defensively.

"Rest? From what could you possibly be resting? That isn't strenuous work, Janet. No, I believe you were deliberately listening in on a conversation, and it isn't the first time." Turning to Sarah, she directed, "Please put away this box of patterns and the fabric, Sarah. Then find the little girls and Steve, and see that they get baths. Janet, come with me."

Leading the way to the living room, she closed the door behind her and had Janet sit on the couch. "I'm going to go find Dad, Janet. He is going to want to talk with you, I'm sure."

"But Mom!" Janet began quickly in a shaky voice. "Really, I didn't do anything wrong! I'm old enough to know what Jeff and Sarah say, especially when they are talking about a wonderful family like the Lockes! After all, Jeff wasn't really fair about James. Dad knows all kinds of good things about him that Jeff didn't even mention. Mr. Locke told Dad that James . . ." Janet suddenly stopped short.

"Yes?" Mom asked. "What did Mr. Locke tell Dad that you heard and no one else did? How would you have heard it, Janet? I think you have quite a bit of explaining to do to your father. You may wait here until he comes." With that, Mom left the room.

In a few minutes, Dad entered the living room with a worried look on his face. He chose a seat next to Janet and quietly sat down. It was a few minutes before he said anything. He seemed to be in deep thought and a slight frown entered his brow.

"Janet," Dad started calmly, "I want you to tell

me everything. I want to hear what you have to say about your listening to Jeff's conversation a few minutes ago. I want to know what you heard Mr. Locke say to me in a private conversation. I want to know why you were listening to that conversation. Let's start with what Mr. Locke said to me, shall we?"

Over the next several minutes, Janet reluctantly told Dad about listening to his conversation with Mr. Locke. Then she told him about Jeff's conversation of a few minutes earlier. Somehow, she didn't feel like arguing with Dad as she had done with Mom earlier. She simply related everything, without much sign of remorse.

When she had finished telling Dad everything she was supposed to, Dad pointedly asked her, "Janet, do you think it is right to listen in on other people's conversations?"

Janet fidgeted a little, but finally meekly answered, "No."

Dad paused a moment. He seemed to be trying to find the best way to say what was coming next.

"Janet, you know that you and I have talked about this problem before, don't you?" Janet silently nodded her head in agreement. "As you know, Sarah is getting old enough to start courtship right now. Someday, some young man is going to be interested in courting you, Janet. And do you know what he is going to do? He is going to ask me about you. What are you really like? What are your character traits? Are there problems you struggle with? What do you think I am going to say? You need to understand right now that I am going to be honest in all of my answers to anyone who wants to court you.

"That will be a few years away, I know," Dad continued. "And no doubt, you will make much progress in the areas you are struggling with right now. But you should know what I would have to answer if I were asked today, right now, about you, Janet. I would have to say that you have a number of areas in which you struggle. I can think of three main areas. I'm going to share them with you now and pray that you will work on them before that time comes. They are all things you and I have talked about many times before.

"First," he began, "you are often guilty of being a busybody in other people's affairs and want to know more than you need to. The problem tonight is a good example of that. Second, you tend to defend yourself instead of admitting you are wrong. The root problem there is just pride. You can't stand to admit that you are wrong. Third, you tend to focus on the way other families conduct their affairs and favor them over the way your own family does things. Your Mom and I have chosen to structure our family life after much prayer and consideration. Yet, you seem to think that our ways are not good, while other families' ways are always good. That kind of a focus could destroy your own marriage, if you are always thinking that someone else's husband has a better idea than the husband God provided for you.

"I'm not trying to scare you, Janet. I love you deeply. I want God to bless you with a wonderful husband and lots of children. But I have to be honest when someone asks me a question. How many men do you think are still going to be interested in courting you after I tell them these things about you?"

Dad gave Janet a big hug. He had tears in his eyes and his voice started to crack. "First, you have to want to change these things. Please, ask God to help you. It is only with His help that you will be able to conquer these things. I struggle with things too, and without God's help I wouldn't be able to begin to make progress on them. Remember that your mom and I love you deeply."

Janet didn't say anything. She just sat there in her dad's embrace with her head bowed low. After a few minutes, Dad got up and walked to the doorway. "Remember, only God can help. We'll be praying for you," he said and walked out.

Chapter Thirteen

$\mathcal{I}$t was a warm Monday in early June when Sarah heard someone knocking on the door. Since she was busy and her hands were covered with bread dough, she called for Steve, who was reading in the living room, to see who was at the door. A few minutes later, Steve came walking quickly through the kitchen on his way out the back door of the house. "Who was it?" Sarah asked, as Steve flew by.

"It's just James," Steve noted. "He told me to get Daddy."

"That's strange," thought Sarah. "I hope nothing is wrong." James always asked for Jeff, not Dad. Maybe it was bad news. Or maybe James wanted to talk some kind of business with Dad, like trading livestock or something. For all Sarah knew, maybe Dad had asked James to come by for some reason. She tried not to think about it and went back to kneading her bread dough.

In a few minutes, Dad came in the back door, wiping the sweat from his forehead with his handkerchief. "Is James here? Steve said he wanted to see me," Dad questioned Sarah.

"I haven't seen him. But I guess Steve told him to wait in the living room, Dad. Do you want me to go get him?" Sarah asked.

"No, I'll go see what he needs," Dad replied.

At least now Sarah knew that Dad had not called for this meeting. It was clear by the puzzled look on his face that Dad didn't know what James wanted to see him about. Hopefully, nothing bad had happened at the Locke farm. Since farm accidents are so common, farmers often fear the worst when someone comes calling unexpectedly. Sarah kept telling herself not to be nosy and just keep her mind on the task at hand.

Dad and James met for a long time. The longer they met, the more curious Sarah became. She tried to think of everything that James could have come calling about. That didn't do anything but confuse her.

Finally, Sarah heard the front door closing and the sound of her Dad walking back to the living room. Why wasn't he going back out to work? Was something wrong? Walking softly to the living room door, she opened it quietly and looked in. There was Dad, kneeling down in front of his chair, apparently praying. She didn't want to interrupt him, so she quietly closed the door and went back to the kitchen. What was going on?

In a few minutes, Dad walked back through the kitchen on his way out the back door. His eyes seemed a little damp and he looked, . . . how could she describe it? Tired. Like he looked after putting up hay all day. Or after he had been splitting firewood all morning. Although she was concerned, Sarah didn't feel like she should say anything to him. It would have been disrespectful for her to feel like she had the right to know everything that Dad did or thought. As he neared the door, he paused, as though trying to decide what to do. Finally, he turned and looked right into Sarah's eyes. Seeing fear and questions in Sarah's eyes, he smiled to put her at ease.

"Sarah, I just had an interesting and important talk with James. He has been praying about something for a long time now. He has discussed it with his father, who, after much prayer, agreed with James." Dad paused and took a breath. Sarah got more tense. This was a strange way to talk. Why didn't Dad just tell her what they had talked about?

"Sarah, James has asked me for permission to court you," Dad finally said. "I'll want to pray about it and talk with Mom before I give him an answer," he quickly added. "The reason I am telling you now, is so that you can pray with us about this matter. It's an important step, Sarah, as I am sure you know."

Sarah was so stunned that when she opened her mouth to speak, no words came out. Dad seemed to understand and came over and gave her a big hug. "We want what is best for you, Sarah. You know that. What is best can be found only by discovering God's will. The only way we can know that is through prayer." He hugged her again, and walked out the door, rubbing his eyes with his handkerchief.

After her conversation with Dad, Sarah hurried up the steps to her bedroom. Finding it empty, she quietly closed the door, then dropped to her knees beside her bed. Her mind and emotions were whirling, and as she glanced down at her folded hands on the quilt, she noticed that they were trembling a little. Sarah smiled to herself and shook her head in amazement.

At last! Someone wanted to court her! Was it really true? Sarah tried to still her thoughts long enough to pray. "Thank you, Lord, thank you! Please help us all to have wisdom and patience, and to know Your will in this. In Jesus' name, Amen."

Sarah felt that her prayer fell short somehow of what it should have been, but she was almost dizzy with excitement. How long she had waited for a Christian young man to show an interest in her. How she had longed for the day when someone would approach her father! Wifehood and motherhood had seemed to be only a dim kind of dream, far in the future, possibly not in the future at all. Now it was a real possibility, and Sarah was so thankful that she whispered again aloud, "Thank you, Father!"

As she slowly calmed down, her thoughts turned to James himself. How nice he was! And she knew he would be a good provider. Wasn't he hard working and dependable? How nice that he and Jeff were friends. A husband who would be close to your brother - how wonderful that would be. Her thoughts continued to whirl for some time.

With a start, Sarah realized that she had been upstairs quite a while. She really should go down and join the rest of the family. Janet had asked her for help with a dress she was sewing, and she had promised to come as soon as she finished the bread. The bread! Uh-oh. Sarah laughed out loud, thinking of what her bread must look like.

Sarah bowed her head against the side of her bed once more before going downstairs, and thanked God for such a wonderful gift as this one.

Chapter Fourteen

During the next week, Sarah seemed to live on a roller-coaster. First, she would be happy and sure that God would lead her and James together. During those times, Sarah found herself thinking not so much of James himself, but more of a vague and shadowy future filled with dreams that had come true. As she helped in the garden, ideas would come unbidden to her mind about her own future garden. Lovely flowers and fragrant herbs, colorful vegetables and bright fruits beckoned to her out of that misty garden. As she cooked meals, visions of a kitchen of her own, and a table set for two people would seem to float into her sight. Sometimes a high chair was also pulled up to the table, and a chubby little hand banged a spoon on the tray.

At other times, Sarah's mind would be filled with doubts. She really didn't know James that well. She knew he had some wonderful character traits, but she really didn't know him. Oh well, that would come during courtship. After all, that's what courtship was for. And even though Dad hadn't given his permission yet for James to court her, likely he would. After all, he thought very highly of Mr. Locke and of James, too, she was sure. Often, thoughts of James and his lack of enjoyment of the younger children would come to Sarah's mind, but she quickly told herself that, after all, they weren't his children. A father would naturally love and enjoy children when they were his own.

One thing that bothered Sarah, however, was her seeming inability to pray. Really deep, true prayer. She did participate in evening family devotions, although nothing was ever said about the possible courtship in front of the rest of the family. In fact, Mom and Dad didn't speak to her at all about the subject, though she knew they were praying about it and she could hear the murmur of their voices behind the closed door of their bedroom each night. Sarah also knelt beside her bed each night, and asked God to give her and her parents wisdom, to know how to answer James. But Sarah rather took it for granted that they would begin the courtship soon, and that then would be the most needed time for prayer.

In one way or another, Jeff, Janet, and Ben learned of Sarah's potential courtship to James. They didn't talk about it much, though, because it seemed that Sarah didn't want to talk about it.

On Sunday, Sarah dressed for church with shaky hands again. In her mind, she scolded herself. "Sarah, keep your thoughts on the sermon this morning and on worshiping God." She prayed for a quiet and calm spirit before the family left the house, and asked God to help her to behave in an appropriate manner.

Sarah wasn't really sure what an appropriate manner was, but she was spared much worry about that anyway. The McLean family arrived just before time for worship to begin and as soon as they were seated, Sarah instinctively glanced over to where the

Lockes always sat. Thankfully, the Lockes were in front of Sarah and to one side, so it would not look obvious for her to gaze in that direction for a brief second.

James seemed to be reading his Bible, and all Sarah saw in that brief glimpse was the back of his head. He was too well-behaved to look around during church, of course, and as soon as the sermon was over, Dad began herding his family toward the door. James did catch Sarah's eyes then, and smiled and waved, but another family was approaching the Lockes to talk, and the McLeans were out the door and on their way home very soon.

At breakfast the following morning, Dad instructed Jeff, Ben, and Steve to work on the pile of lumber next to the barn that seemed to always be in a state of dishevelment. "Sort it by size and quality," he instructed. "If you find any rotten stuff, throw it on the burn pile. Think you can handle that boys?"

"Yes!" were the enthusiastic replies. Steve and Ben always enjoyed the chance to do "real work" with Jeff.

Mom had written a list of things for Rachel and Becky to work on. "Please start sorting the laundry first," she told them. "I need to get it started right away. And Janet, I need you to make some good progress on that dress you're making. It seems like it has been days since you worked on it."

Soon everyone was off, starting their assigned chores with singing and laughing. Sarah stayed in the kitchen cleaning up the pans that were used to make eggs. They were kind of hard to clean and Sarah liked to do them herself instead of having Rachel or Janet do them. She liked to make sure they were totally clean, not just "almost clean." In a few minutes, Dad came back into the kitchen.

"Sarah, can you come into the living room for a minute?" he asked.

When Sarah entered the living room, she saw her mother sitting on the couch, looking as though she had bad news of some kind. "Oh, no, not something wrong with the baby!" Sarah feared. But Dad soon revealed the purpose of the meeting.

"Sarah, as you know, James has asked permission to court you," he began.

Sarah smiled instinctively and sat on the very edge of her seat. She was relieved there was nothing wrong with Mom or her baby. She had been wondering how long it would be before her parents officially gave their permission for her to consider courting James. Now it was finally time.

Dad looked a little pained when Sarah displayed her happy, expectant attitude. "Well, your Mom and I have prayed about this for a week now. I'm sure you have too," he added.

Sarah nodded silently, but felt a little guilty. "I have prayed," she kept telling herself. "So why do I feel a little guilty? I'm not lying."

"I have also had several visits with James, at his house, where we talked about many things," Dad continued. "I had a long conversation with Mr. Locke on Saturday morning that lasted close to three hours. I want to share with you some of what I have learned and what I have decided. But first, I would like to pray." Dad got on his knees and lead in a prayer. While he was praying, Sarah's mind was racing. This didn't seem to be going like she thought it would.

"Sarah, you know how much Mom and I love you. You know we want the best for you and only want what is God's will," Dad started. "James is a nice young man. I think he is growing as a Christian and desires to follow Christ in his life. He has taken a real interest in you, as I told you last week. I believe that in time, with the grace of God working in his life, James will make someone a good husband."

Dad paused. He was having trouble putting his thoughts into words. "In the course of observing James, talking with him on many occasions, and talking with his father, I have learned a lot about him. Like I said, many things about him are good. Unfortunately, he has a few areas of his life which are not where they need to be. This is difficult to talk about, because we all have things in our lives that need work. I feel God has given me the responsibility, though, of looking carefully at any man who desires to court you.

"James has a problem when it comes to children, Sarah. He says he likes children, but then he says that he doesn't want too many children. James said that he didn't feel it was necessary to have lots of kids in order to have a good marriage. He also said that he often gets irritated, even angry, when he has to watch small children for any length of time because of their childish ways. He was quick to add that he thought his views on children would change just as soon as he had some of his own. I'm afraid I am not convinced that's true. I have seen the way he treats his younger sisters and other children. He is just not fond of children. It is possible that he can change that area of his life, although I must admit that it would take a mighty work of the Holy Spirit and James' desire to change to bring it about. And in all of my dealings I have not sensed any desire on his part to change his feelings toward children.

If that were all, I might still have been able to allow him to court you. Unfortunately, I have learned other things about James, from his father, which make him an unsuitable candidate for courtship at this time. Those things I cannot share, not even with you, Sarah, and I apologize for that. You will just have to trust me on them. I can tell you that in evaluating James, I spent a lot of time looking at the qualifications for elders found in I Timothy. I know he's not ready to be an elder, but it is a good study in what a mature Christian man should be like.

"I'm sorry to say that I can't give my permission for James to court you." Dad reached over and hugged Sarah, tears welling up in his eyes. Mom, crying aloud, was hugging Sarah also. "I don't know what God has in store for you. It could be that James will make major changes in his life and will then come and ask to court you again. If he does and there is evidence of a changed attitude and life, then I will certainly reconsider. I'm sorry, honey. I know how much you want to find a husband and start your life together. But it needs to be the right one." At this Dad broke down and cried, and Sarah, who had been holding her emotions in, suddenly started too.

After a few minutes, Sarah regained her composure and said, "I do love you, Mom and Dad. I do know that you want what is best for me. I know it has been hard for you to make this decision. It's just that I was so hoping this could be the one and then I could..." she stopped talking, and started crying again. Mom and Dad continued to hug her.

Finally, Sarah said, "I think I'm okay now." She was no longer crying, but was sniffling. "I would like to go to my room if that's okay. I'll finish the dishes later, Mom."

"Don't worry about the dishes," Dad said. "Let's pray before you go. God, please bless Sarah and fill her with Your love and compassion. Help her to know of our love for her. Help her to trust You to bring the right young man into her life. Please give me wisdom as I have such hard decisions to make for her. Above all things, we desire Your will to be done. In Jesus' name. Amen."

As Sarah left the room, Dad looked at Mom. "Is it always going to be this hard?" he asked.

"Let's pray it won't," was Mom's reply. "When will you tell James?"

"I meet with him at noon today. I'm not looking forward to it. Pray for me, won't you?"

Chapter Fifteen

When Sarah arrived at her room, she noticed that no one was in it. In fact, no other children seemed to be around anywhere. Finally she realized what had happened. Mom and Dad had given chores to each of the other children so they would be away for a while. "How thoughtful," Sarah gratefully reflected.

Her demeanor, while sad, was still not totally downcast. She reflected on the words of Dad and Mom. Oh, how blessed she felt to have such good, loving parents. It was obvious that it hurt them as much as it did her to have to tell her the news. And yet they were willing to go through that, rather than take the easy course and just let Sarah learn about James the hard way later. "I just hope I have half as much love and compassion for my children as they have for me," Sarah whispered to herself.

At this point she felt led to get on her knees and offer a prayer of gratitude for her parents. As she prayed, she also asked God to make James the man that God would have him to be. She prayed that James would be nice when Dad gave him the news. She then asked God to supply the right wife for James. Finally, she prayed that God would give her parents and her wisdom about any young men who wanted to court her in the future.

As she rose to her feet, her thoughts remained

on the idea of future courtship. She crossed to the window and sat on the edge of Janet's bed, looking out over the hay fields in the distance. Some were a long way away. Was that "how far away" she was from finding a husband?

Who was going to court her now? She didn't know any young men about her age that would be suitable candidates. Where were they supposed to come from? It had seemed so providential when James had moved to the community with his family. Wasn't that the hand of God moving in a mysterious way to bring about a match for Sarah? At least, she had thought so until only an hour ago.

The longer she sat there, the more she began to question. Dad had told her about James not particularly liking or respecting children. Well, that wasn't exactly news to her. But she had thought that all out this past week. It's just because they weren't his own children. Surely he would love, respect, and cherish his own children. She didn't know of any fathers who didn't do that! In a way, it seemed unfair that this should be an issue to cause their courtship to be stopped even before it began. Why, it's even possible that during the courtship itself, with the loving example of Jeff always in front of him, James would change his opinions of children. Yes, that was very possible! That's what courtship was for, wasn't it? Not just learning about someone, but also helping them to start making changes where needed.

Sarah started feeling quite discontented and sorry for herself. She reflected that these feelings were only natural. How could she help how she felt? She wondered if Dad had considered the same thoughts she just had. Did he realize that the man, and even Sarah, might change during the courtship in positive ways? She started wondering if she should approach Dad with these thoughts. It was just too important not to tell him.

As she stood up, she thought about what else Dad had said. Something about James having a few other areas of his life that were not what they should be. Dad didn't want to tell her what those were. She understood that Dad didn't want to be a busybody and spread news of James' character flaws. She knew he was right, and was actually thankful that Dad didn't just reveal all of the negative things he had learned about James. That proved that Dad was meek and gentle. But surely he knew that Sarah wouldn't run and tell everyone what she had heard about James! Why couldn't he have at least listed, without going into detail, what James' flaws were? Then she could pray for them, specifically!

Yes, she felt that Dad needed to hear some of these thoughts and she started out the door to go find him while they were still fresh on her mind. As she was almost out the door, her eyes fell on a bright yellow piece of construction paper, with torn corners and messy writing, lying in the floor right in front of her. She stooped down, instinctively, to pick it up, and smiled a little. It was a Bible verse scrawled on the paper. Several of the "e's" were facing backward and the name "Rachel" was written in bold letters about four times larger than the verse. But what really stopped Sarah was when she took the time to decipher the verse written there: "Honor thy father and thy mother, that thy days may be long upon the earth."

Tears starting welling up in Sarah's eyes. Tears of love and of regret. Regret that she had almost let herself confront Dad about something that he had obviously prayed for and struggled with for over a week. Regret that she had determined to go and set him straight on a few facts. "Oh, God, why am I so sinful?" Sarah prayed right there standing by the door. "Help me to honor my father and my mother. Help me to do Your will, not my own."

As she walked down the stairs to the kitchen, Sarah no longer had any intention of confronting Mom or Dad. She was resolved to trust fully in their decisions and humbly obey. That was God's will for her life.

Turning into the kitchen, though, the thought popped into her head again. But, was it the best decision? Unfortunately, that was a thought she was going to have to struggle with for some time to come.

That evening, Becky seemed to be having a lot of trouble going to sleep. Sarah got out of bed and walked quietly over to Becky's side. "What's wrong, Becky? Are you hot?"

"I think I saw a tall man wearing a green coat walking on the ceiling," said Becky, her big blue eyes staring at the ceiling.

Sarah looked up at the ceiling, more to make Becky feel that Sarah was really looking for the man than anything else. Looking back down at Becky she said, "There's nothing up there, honey. I'm sure it was just a dream. Now, why don't you just turn over and go to sleep. I'm here with you and won't let anything happen to you. I promise."

Becky calmed down a little and looked at Sarah. "I'm glad you're my sister. I really don't have to be afraid, though," she added, "even if you get up and go to the bathroom or something. Mommy taught me a verse: 'What time I am afraid I will trust in Thee.' That means I can trust in God if I get afraid. That's nice, isn't it, Sarah?"

As Sarah returned to her own bed, she realized that Becky was right! She was so afraid of not finding a husband. That fear was as real to Sarah as Becky's fear of the tall man on the ceiling. In both cases, they must trust in God. Sarah once again prayed and asked God to give her the faith to trust Him about the future. Although she had dreaded going to bed for fear of not being able to sleep, in a few minutes she was sound asleep.

One week had passed since Dad had revealed his decision to Sarah. Sarah was sitting on the porch in the swing, silently thinking about James. She had never said anything to Dad or Mom and had tried to smile when she saw them, even though sometimes her efforts had been weak. She knew they were hurting along with her and didn't want to make it any harder on them. Still, it was impossible not to think of James and what might have been. It had been hard to see him in church on Sunday. Although she hadn't spoken to him, James seemed to be sad, too.

While she gently swung on the porch, deep in thought, Ben was quietly carving a piece of hickory on the steps with his pocket knife. Ben seemed to read

Sarah's thoughts, perhaps because he was often thinking and silent himself. God had given him a quiet, reflective personality, often wise beyond his years. After a while, Ben got up, stretched, and walked over closer to where Sarah was sitting. Speaking softly, almost too softly for even her to hear, Ben began, "You know Sarah, you don't want a husband that's just okay and kind of meets the basics. You want one that is special . . . like Dad. One you can depend on and trust completely, even to make all the decisions for the family . . . " he paused, searching for the right example, " . . . like Mom can trust Dad. And one your children can look up to, and your sons can have as a living example of what a godly man should be . . . you know, like Jeff and Steve and I can follow Dad." He continued carving, as he had done while he spoke. Never during his discourse had he even looked at Sarah. It was almost as if he were talking to himself.

What brought that on? wondered Sarah. Surely, Ben can't read my mind and know what I'm thinking. Such a long discourse for Ben was impossible to ignore, however. Sarah knew it was a deep, heartfelt conviction that made him speak to her. After another minute, Sarah quietly spoke, "Thanks Ben." Ben didn't respond, but Sarah hadn't expected him to.

Ten minutes later, Steve came running up to the porch. "Want to go fishing, Ben? I'll bet they're biting about now!" Without saying anything, Ben closed his knife, and walked off the porch in the direction of the shed where the fishing poles were kept.

No sooner had he left, than Becky came out on the porch to rock her baby doll. Sarah was a little alarmed because Becky had red eyes. Right away, though, Becky confided in her big sister, "Daddy just gave me a spanking. I got angry at Rachel because she was looking at my doll; so I tried to hit her with the big serving spoon I was drying. Daddy spanked me, then gave me a big hug and held me in his lap."

Becky sat down in the swing next to Sarah and held her doll closely. "Now, now, you know it's time for your nap. Why don't you just give it up and close your eyes? Mommy will sing to you, okay?" Becky sang softly to her doll and held it tight. A smile came to her lips and she said, "Sarah, you know what? I think Jesus and Daddy must be the kindest people in the whole world."

Suddenly, it was as though a surge of electricity went through Sarah's heart. She realized clearly, for the first time, that James was not the one for her. Sarah wanted her own little girl to someday be able to say, "I think Jesus and Daddy must be the kindest people in the world."

As Sarah was thinking these thoughts and was about to go and find Dad, Mom called through the screen door. "Sarah? Could you walk out to the mailbox for me? The mailman just went by and Jeff is expecting a part for his tractor. My hands are covered in bread dough, so if you would go and check the box I'd appreciate it."

"Sure, Mom," Sarah smiled. "I'll take Becky with me. Come on, Becky, want to help me get the mail?"

"Goody! Can I carry the mail back to Mommy? Please, Sarah?"

"We'll see. Maybe there will be something you can carry." Sarah held Becky's hand and they started down the porch steps.

"Wait Sarah, please! My baby is crying. She wants to go with us!" Becky picked up her doll and patted her back, comforting her. Then she said to her baby, "Well, you're pretty little to carry any mail, but we'll see."

Sarah smiled at her, trying hard not to laugh, and they started off again. At the box, they found a letter for Mom and Dad from the Williams family. The girls walked back to the house and Becky put the letter on the table for Mommy and Daddy.

After supper Dad said, "Let's get the chores done quickly if we want to build that campfire tonight. I have an interesting letter to share with you. And did you get some marshmallows today, Sarah?"

"I sure did," Sarah answered with a smile.

"Hooray!" shouted Becky, Rachel and Steve in unison.

Chapter Sixteen

Later that evening at the campfire, everyone had fun looking at the stars, eating marshmallows, and playing "sparks alive" with burning sticks from the fire. After awhile, Dad asked everyone to listen up for a minute. "I thought you might like to hear an interesting letter we received today," Dad began. "It's from the Williams family. They are a wonderful, godly family who are old friends of ours. Many years ago, when Sarah and Jeff were small, we lived in the same town and attended the same church. Both our family and theirs have moved twice since then, and they are living in Pennsylvania now. We keep in touch occasionally by mail, but I suppose it's been ten or twelve years since we've seen them, wouldn't you say Kate?" Mom nodded.

"Williams . . . is that the family who had five boys before they had a girl, Mom?" Janet asked.

"Yes, it is!" Mom laughed. "I remember how excited Carol was to have a girl after all those boys, too. And Carol Williams was the one who taught me how to make homemade bread many years ago. She is such a sweet friend." Mom paused a moment, thinking of Carol. "Her husband Mark is a fine Christian man - one of the kindest and gentlest people I have ever met."

"He really is," agreed Dad. "I always enjoyed

Mark's company. Perhaps that's why we've kept in touch all these years. I think I probably have more respect for the Williams than for any other family I've ever known, and we have known many fine Christian families. Well, shall I read the letter now?" finished Dad.

"Please! Oh yes, yes!" exclaimed several of the younger children. "We promise to be quiet." Dad read the letter:

> Dear Kate, David, and Children,
>
> Greetings in Jesus' name. It was good to hear from you last winter, as always. Reading your letters always makes us wish we could see you again - it has been so many years, yet your friendship is still very precious to us.
>
> The Lord has blessed us in many ways this year, which we hope to tell you more about later. Our biggest news right now is that we plan to make a long hoped-for visit to you at the end of August. Our oldest son, Luke, has spent three years apprenticing with both a carpenter and a plumber in our local fellowship here. One of the elders in our church has a brother who is a general contractor close to your area, and he has asked Luke to come and work with him. We met Mr. Taylor when he was here visiting his brother last winter, and he is a Christian man who we

believe will be kind and fair to Luke.

It will be hard for us to let Luke go so far away, but we have prayed about it, as Luke has, and believe the Lord's hand is in this. It will be a little easier knowing that he will be fairly close to your family - about an hour away, I think.

We will be moving Luke and his few earthly possessions to his new location the last few days of August. We thought that if it is agreeable to you, we would come for a visit on the 28th. We'll stay the 29th also, then the morning of the 30th we will need to go on to his new place, so that he will be ready to begin his new job September 1.

If these plans will work out for you, please let us know. If not, we will certainly understand. I know you will have a new baby to care for by then, Lord willing. We certainly do not want to be a burden. We will gladly stay in a motel if that is best for you.

We look forward to hearing from you, and especially to seeing you soon. We pray God's grace and safe-keeping on your dear family.

In Christ's love,
Carol, Mark, and Children

No one was quiet for long. Excited questions flew from the children about the names and ages of the Williams' children, what activities they might enjoy during their visit, and what sleeping arrangements they could make. Steve was disappointed that they wouldn't be coming during ice-skating weather, since ice-skating was one of his favorite activities and he was convinced that everyone enjoyed it as much as he did.

"Well," Dad laughed, "I don't believe you'll find much ice in August, Steve. But we do have a tent and perhaps some of their boys would enjoy camping in the yard with you."

"Could we, Dad? That would be so much fun!" Steve exclaimed.

"And it would give us much more room in the house," added Mom. "Oh, but look at the time. It is past time for little ones to be in bed. Tell Dad good night now, please. Then right into the house. Don't forget to get your water and go to the bathroom."

The month of July was busy for Sarah. She was glad for all the activity and glad to see the beginning of the harvest season again. Strawberries had already been made into jam and now blueberries were ready. Sarah knew it wouldn't be long before it was time for raspberries, with peaches, pears, and corn right behind. She and Janet were kept busy all day, every day, harvesting vegetables from the garden, drying herbs, and teaching the little girls to help as much as they were able. There was quite a bit they could do now, with Rachel being six and Becky four and a half. Dad had made the little girls a low clothesline of their own, and they were able to hang small items by themselves, then fold and put away that part of the laundry.

The month flew by, and Sarah realized with a small pang one day that her little sisters would not always be little. Of course, she had really known that already, but as she watched them pick wildflowers and play in the sandbox, the Lord seemed to open her eyes. She was reminded of how only a few years ago, Rachel and Becky were just babies. Sarah and Janet had often taken turns keeping them occupied and helping Mom work in the garden or kitchen.

Sarah's thoughts turned to the new baby, due very soon now. If God sent a young man to be her husband in the next few years, she would miss seeing this baby grow up. There would be a little brother or sister playing here who wouldn't be able to run to Sarah in excitement, to share some new little discovery. Suddenly, a lump came to Sarah's throat. She still hoped for marriage and a home of her own, but perhaps it would be a bit easier to wait for God's timing, remembering that. She had a very happy home and life now, and once she was gone, it would never be quite the same again.

Chapter Seventeen

The evening had been unusually warm, even for early August, and Sarah had tossed and turned for quite awhile before falling asleep.

It seemed she hadn't been asleep long at all before someone was gently shaking her shoulder. "Sarah, Sarah," Dad was whispering. "Wake up, Sarah."

Drowsily, Sarah opened her eyes, still not fully awake. "Huh? What? Dad?"

"Sarah, we need you. Wake up please. Mom's in labor, and the midwife is on her way."

Suddenly Sarah was wide awake, and could see a soft light coming from under her parents' closed bedroom door across the hall. She looked over at her little sisters, sleeping soundly in their beds on the other side of the room and wondered what time it was. Pulling a light cotton robe over her gown, she followed Dad to the softly lit bedroom and gazed down at Mom, who was lying very still with her eyes closed, breathing slowly and deeply. After a few seconds, Mom gave a small sigh and opened her eyes.

"Sarah." Mom said her name so quietly that Sarah was not even sure she had really spoken. Kneeling beside the bed, Sarah's worried face looked into Mom's calm one.

"Are you okay, Mom? Is everything all right? What should I do?"

Mom reached out for Sarah's hand, gave it a gentle squeeze, then suddenly closed her eyes and lay very still, breathing slowly and deeply once again. After nearly a full minute, she sighed again and opened her eyes. "The baby will be here really soon," Mom told Dad and Sarah. "Better get ready quickly. Do whatever Dad says, Sarah." She tried to smile at Sarah but couldn't, and Sarah found herself wishing that Mom hadn't even tried to smile.

Mom almost didn't seem like Mom, and Sarah was just a little frightened. She looked up at Dad, and fear must have shown on her face, for Dad reached out a strong sure hand to help her up. Then in a reassuring voice he said, "Sarah, Mom is fine. I've seen her through this many times before. She has some pain, but not lots. It will be over soon and, as she always says, it certainly is worth it to hold a sweet new baby in your arms. But I don't think the midwife will make it, and we need to work fast."

Sarah nodded her head and he gave her quick directions which she promptly and rather shakily obeyed. Just fifteen minutes later, Sarah was holding her new baby brother in her arms as Dad ran downstairs to let the midwife in the front door.

Anne, Mom's sweet, smiling midwife, came into the room, bringing a calm assurance with her for which Sarah would have been even more grateful a bit earlier. After checking the baby and Mom over, and pronouncing them doing fine, she turned to Sarah. "You did a great job helping your parents, Sarah," she smiled. "If you ever decide you'd like to be a midwife, perhaps I could interest you in being my apprentice."

"Thanks," Sarah smiled back. "I think right

now I'm just grateful to the Lord that Mom and the baby are okay. I'm not really ready to go through this again anytime soon," she sighed. "Maybe I'll feel differently after I've calmed down a little, though."

Anne laughed understandingly and gave Sarah's shoulders a quick hug. Turning toward the door, she beckoned to Jeff, who was waiting in the doorway. "Come on in and meet your new sibling," she told him. "I'll go downstairs and fix some glasses of juice for everyone. I think your Dad plans to bring the rest of the crew in, too."

Jeff took the baby, nestled it gently in his arms, and began to speak softly to him. Here was this big, strong young man who could throw hay bales all day long, hardly seeming to tire. Yet he was so tender, so loving, so careful with his new brother that it brought tears to Sarah's eyes.

She looked at the clock and was surprised to see that it was nearly six a.m. Sarah had been so sleepy when Dad woke her up, then so concerned about Mom, that she had failed to notice that the sky had been getting light as she got out of her bed. The air was much cooler this morning, she noticed, and there was a slight breeze coming into the bedroom from the open windows. A beautiful day for her little brother's birthday, she thought to herself. Then, before she gave the baby back to Mom, she closed her eyes and thanked God for His precious new gift in her arms.

Before too long, the other children started streaming into the bedroom. Little four-year-old Becky, who wasn't quite sure about all of this, cautiously made her way into the room, looking in all the corners like there might be something or someone hiding there.

When she saw her new baby brother, though, she let out a squeal of delight. "Just look at those little hands! Those tiny, tiny little hands! How cute!"

Rachel sure didn't have any fears as she entered the bedroom. In fact, she came flying into the room and was about to jump on the bed with Mommy, when Daddy quickly said, "Whoa there gal! Let's slow down a little. We sure don't want to hurt him, do we?" Then directing her to the side of the bed, he added, "See, you can see him from the side, like this."

Rachel was very excited, and asked, "What's his name, Daddy? Can I hold him? Daddy, please can I hold him?"

"Sure you can. You both can," he said to Becky and Rachel. "And his name is Samuel. All I ask is that you be very, very careful with him. He's just a little guy as you can see. He can't hold his head up, so we have to hold him like this, see?" Dad said, demonstrating the proper technique to the excited girls.

When Rachel had the baby in her arms, she let out another squeal of delight. Now this was fine for the older people in the room, but the baby didn't think it was too great. He puckered up his red, little face and started crying loudly. Rachel, looking a little confused and worried, asked Daddy, "Now what do I do?"

"Well, you can try to rock back and forth with him. Carefully. Real carefully. That's right. Remember to support his neck . . . That's good! . . . See, he's starting to calm down for you. You're going to be a good mommy someday, Rachel."

Rachel beamed. She liked having a new baby brother. Remembering her lessons on sharing, she turned to Becky and said, "Do you want to hold him now? I've got him good and calmed down."

"Yes!" said Becky.

"Let's have you sit down in this chair, Becky," Daddy said. "There, that's good. Now, support his neck. Good! Kate, can you see how well Becky is doing? You're learning quickly, Becky! You're going to be a good mommy too, someday." Becky had a big smile on her face.

"He sure is cute!" Becky noted matter-of-factly. "When did he arrive? I thought I heard the front door opening a little while ago. Is that when he got here?"

"Yes, that's about when he came," Dad said with a smile and a wink to Sarah.

"I thought so," Becky said, feeling so grown-up and important.

By that time, Ben, Steve, and Janet had also entered the room and they took turns holding their new brother. Everyone was excited, as can be imagined, and the noise level got louder and louder. No one was trying to be loud. It just turned out that way. After a minute or so, Dad said, "Okay, troops. That's about all the noise and excitement that Samuel and Mommy need right now. He'll be living here quite a while and we'll all get a chance to see him lots more. For now, let's go downstairs and let them rest. I want Janet and Jeff to start getting breakfast ready. Ben and Steve, you go start chores. And Rachel and Becky, I want you to be making beds while breakfast is getting put on the table. Sarah, you can get dressed or just rest for a while, if you're tired. I'll be downstairs in a minute."

Everyone left the room except Dad, Mom and the new baby. Dad held Mom's hand and spent a few minutes just looking from Mom to the new baby. Joy and gratitude were written all over his face. Tears welled up in his eyes and he said, voice breaking, "God has blessed us again, Kate. God has blessed us again." It was all he could get out, but Kate understood. There were tears in her eyes, too.

Chapter Eighteen

It was the 28th of August, and the morning was quite warm. The day had started much like any other day, with everyone getting up and eating breakfast early. After lunch, the boys had gone out to do the afternoon chores. Then the day suddenly became more exciting than most.

"The calves are out! The calves are out!" shouted Steve, running into the house through the back door. "They're everywhere! Come on everybody! We have to get them before they head to the highway!" Steve was never one to remain calm, but today his excitement seemed justified. Stories of the accidents that occur on highways when cars and calves mix themselves together are not happy ones.

Everyone rushed out of the house to help. Even Becky and Rachel grabbed a rope and headed toward the barn area. Only Mom and baby Samuel stayed behind, although Samuel seemed ready to join in the fun and excitement by the way he stared after the rushing mob. "You'll have to wait a few years, big boy, before you can help out," Mom said. "Let's go check your diaper."

It was the usual mayhem that occurs when calves, who have been dreaming of escaping past the confines of their fences, suddenly have new-found freedom. They simply don't know where to go or what to do. As a result, they run everywhere and do everything they can think of. Legs were kicking up in the air, calves were snorting and bawling, and the crazy group charged anything and everything they found in their path.

Dad soon had his "army" of children in position to control the mob. He placed the smaller girls well out of harm's way, but still where they could be of assistance closing and latching gates. "Okay, let's move in slowly, and try to get them to move to the west a little . . . Not so fast Steve! Don't rush them or they will just run right past us . . . That's better . . . There they go. Slowly, . . . slowly." The calves seemed to be ready to be captured.

Suddenly, one calf realized what was happening and bolted through an opening between Janet and Sarah. "Try to close him off," Dad called. They tried, but the calf had other ideas. The result was that Janet ended up on the ground, manure and dirt staining her dress.

"Are you okay, Janet?" Dad asked anxiously.

"I'm fine," Janet answered. "Just lost my footing trying to turn too quickly."

This kind of "battle" continued for quite some time. Before it was all over, everyone was hot, sweaty, and several had manure and dirt stains on their dresses or pants. Sarah had even somehow managed to get manure in her hair and on the left side of her face. "I suppose we should just be thankful that they didn't make it to the highway and that no one got hurt," was Dad's summary of the situation. "Let's get to the house and clean up some."

Coming around the house, they came face to

face with a large family walking up the driveway. A clean family, with clean clothes and clean faces. "Mark!" Dad shouted and ran to greet his friend of so many years. "Welcome folks! My, what a welcome sight you are!" And then looking down at his clothes and looking at his children, he laughed. "And what a sight we are! We decided to get all dressed up for your visit. And you got here just in time!"

Everyone laughed. Then Dad briefly explained about the calves getting out. "Say, if you had just been here about an hour ago and joined in the fun, I'll bet we could have gotten those calves back into their pen in, . . . oh, around two hours, instead of one!"

"David, you haven't changed a bit!" Mark laughed. "I've missed your sense of humor all these years. It sure is good to see you again."

"Well, let's not stand here baking in the sun. Why don't we move into the house?" Dad suggested. "The children and I can get cleaned up in a jiffy and meanwhile, you can greet the newest blessing from God to our family." Everyone walked into the house. Sarah was embarrassed at the way she must have looked, but what could she do?

Mom was coming down the stairs with a sleepy Samuel in her arms as the Williams entered the kitchen. "Oh, hello!" she exclaimed. "It's so good to see you all! Mark, Carol, you are a real blessing to have here," Mom said happily. "But I'm afraid I can't recognize a single one of your children!" she finished with a laugh. "While everyone else gets cleaned up, why don't you all sit down and let me get you a cold drink. Then we'll only have to introduce everyone once. Would you like to hold the baby for me?" she asked Carol Williams.

"Would I!" Carol exclaimed. "It's been four years since I've had one this small. How I've missed it."

Soon the rest of the McLeans came into the kitchen for a cold drink also, and the fathers introduced their families to each other. Sarah thought she would have a hard time remembering all the boys' names, but she knew right away that she liked them all. Luke would be easy to remember, since he was the one they had heard about the most. At 21, he seemed quite mature, but also easy-going and as friendly as his dad. Andrew, at 18, was taller than Luke. Andrew reminded Sarah a little of her brother Ben - still a nice friendly person, but quieter and more reserved. Daniel was 16, and he looked just like his father must have looked at the same age. Matthew and Jonathan, at 14 and 11, she would have to learn more about later. As soon as they finished their lemonade, they took off with Ben and Steve for the creek.

The Williams' girls were Anna, Hope, and little Beth. Beth was four, and very quiet and shy. She sat on her mother's lap with a doll in her arms. Sarah knew that once Beth warmed up, she and Becky would get along fine. Anna and Hope were nine and seven, and they were kneeling on either side of Samuel's cradle in a corner of the kitchen. Rachel was eagerly telling them of all the things she was able to do, helping take care of her new baby brother. Anna and Hope seemed to both be happy little girls with quick, bright smiles, and it seemed to Sarah that they would be very well-behaved and cheerful playmates for Rachel. "Mom and Dad were right about the Williams," Sarah reflected silently. "They are a wonderful, godly family. I already have a lot of respect for them myself."

Soon the two families broke into smaller groups to explore the house and farm, Janet and Sarah were left alone in the kitchen to wash up the glasses and begin cooking supper. "The Williams are so nice!" began Janet enthusiastically. "I think they are one of the nicest families we've ever met."

Sarah laughed. "I think you're right this time, Janet," she agreed. "I'm sure we're going to have a wonderful visit."

Later, after everyone had finished eating, Luke Williams spoke up. "Since the McLean girls cooked the meal and Mrs. McLean has a baby to take care of, how about the guys cleaning up? The parents could have a chance to visit alone, and with all of us efficient guys working, it shouldn't take long."

"Why Luke, that is really kind of you. And even if you did volunteer all of the other boys, I believe we'll accept very quickly, before anyone can back out," Mom laughed.

"Maybe eight guys would be a few too many working in the kitchen at one time, though," suggested Dad, "so Ben and Steve, why don't you let Matthew and Jonathan help you do the evening chores?"

"Okay, Dad. Then could we set up the tent?" Ben asked eagerly.

"Sure," Dad replied. "The older guys in the kitchen will probably be able to help you by then." Since everything was set, the younger boys headed out to the barn.

Sarah and Janet held a whispered conference with their mother in the hallway before she went into the living room. "We'll get the beds ready, Mom," offered Janet. "Sarah and I thought we'd better get started. This may take awhile! Where do we put everybody?"

"Thank you, girls," smiled Mom. "I believe we'll let the older boys stay in the boys' room, so we'll need a sleeping bag on the floor for Jeff in there. The four younger boys will be in the tent, and they'll be able to get their own sleeping bags out. Mr. and Mrs. Williams can sleep on the pull-out couch in the living room, and all the little girls can sleep in the girls' room. I guess we'll need another sleeping bag in there for Rachel."

"That only leaves Janet and me out in the cold, Mom," Sarah said. "Or maybe I should say out in the heat. Where do we sleep?"

"Oh, I'm sorry girls!" exclaimed Mom. "Well, let's see. I guess you'll have to make pallets on the floor out of blankets, and then sleep either on the kitchen floor, or move things around in the sewing room. Be sure to get an alarm clock so that you can get up early to start the muffins." Mom gave them each a quick hug, then went to join the others in the living room.

Seating herself in the rocker with Samuel, Mom smiled over at Carol, who was listening quietly as their husbands discussed Luke's new job. "It's a fine opportunity for him, David," Mark was saying. "Evan Taylor has no children of his own and his brother, Bill, an elder in our church, feels that Luke is an answer to prayer for him. Evan and his wife have been looking forward all summer to having Luke come. Bill believes that Luke is capable and mature enough to become a partner with Evan in a few years. And as we wrote you, Evan Taylor is a fine Christian man who we feel will be fair to Luke."

"His wife, Nancy, is really nice too," added Carol. "I know she'll be inviting Luke over for some home-cooked meals. I just hope he won't be too homesick," she finished quietly.

Mom reached a hand over to Carol and gave her arm a gentle squeeze. "Luke is certainly welcome to come and spend some weekends with us," she reassured Mrs. Williams. "I know he and Jeff are going to be good friends - they seem to be so much alike. And it would be difficult to feel lonely around here!" she added cheerfully. "Just let him try to find a quiet minute alone."

"That's right," Dad agreed. "Why, Ben and Steve alone would occupy all Luke's time, begging him to go fishing in the creek with them. And the little girls are always needing an extra brother or two to fix everything they manage to break."

"Well, I'm thankful the Lord provided this opportunity for Luke so close to your family," remarked Mr. Williams. "It will keep us from worrying about him. Isn't that right, Carol? You're not going to worry about Luke?"

"If you say so, dear," smiled Mrs. Williams

Chapter Nineteen

The next few weeks were as busy as they always were at this time of year. The gathering and canning of produce were made especially fun since little baby Samuel's noises were always nearby. Even putting up the last bales of hay didn't seem so hard this year, knowing that a sweet little baby would be cooing at you soon. In many ways it just seemed that life couldn't get any better.

This time of year, with everyone working closely together for long periods of time, lent itself to lots of long conversations. And the McLean family, it seemed, never ran out of things to talk about.

"Weren't the Williams so nice?" asked Janet, for about the tenth time since their visit. "Their boys are so kind and their dad is just about as funny as Dad! Did I tell you that Luke walked in once when I was trying to scrub off some burned-on food in our biggest pot and actually asked if he could try his hand at getting it off?"

"Yes, I think you did, dear," Mom replied, smiling. "They sure were nice boys and their daughters were nice also. That little Beth has the sweetest, chubbiest cheeks I think I've ever seen! I could hardly keep from reaching over and patting them every time she walked through the room."

"Now, how old was Jonathan?" Steve asked.

"He was eleven," Janet answered.

"Oh, yeah, that's right." Steve said. "I get their ages all mixed up. There are so many of them to keep up with!"

"Well," said Mom, laughing, "no more than we have in our family. But I do know what you mean. Trying to learn everyone's ages and names at one time can be a little confusing, even for me."

Four-year-old Becky started giggling to herself and covered her mouth.

"What's so funny?" asked Janet.

"Oh, it's nothing," but Becky giggled some more. "I was standing behind a tree pretending to be a stage coach driver when Jonathan came out the back door." She couldn't repress more giggles. "He didn't see me. He looked and I guess he saw that everyone was in the barn or something. Anyway, he looked around first, then started running toward the barn." At this, she broke out in laughs. "He ran so funny, Janet! His legs did funny things when he ran! They kind of flopped back and forth. He looked so funny! Kind of like a chicken or something."

"Becky," Mom said seriously, "you didn't laugh at him, did you? Did he see you laugh at him?"

"I don't know," Becky said, a little frightened. "I don't remember."

"Honey, you need to know that Jonathan can't help the way he runs," Mom said softly. "He was born with a problem in his legs. The doctors weren't even sure that he would ever be able to walk, much less run. You see," she continued, "it's a miracle from God that he can even walk or run at all. His legs will never work like yours, Becky. Never. That's the best he can do. I think he is a little embarrassed about it too, so we don't want to laugh about it. Some people can't help the way they walk, or talk, or look. We need to remember that God loves them anyway and so should we. And we don't want to laugh at them because that can make them feel bad. Okay?"

Tears were almost in Becky's eyes. "Okay, Mommy," she said. "I didn't know."

"I know you didn't," Mom smiled and hugged Becky. "It's just one of those things you have to learn in life. Now, you'll be more careful when you see someone who looks 'kind of funny' or different, won't you?"

"Yes ma'am," said Becky seriously. Then, with enthusiasm, "Say, why don't I make him a card! I could say I'm sorry and draw him a picture and everything!"

"That's a sweet idea, Becky," Mom said. "Why don't you draw him a card, but not say anything about laughing at him? He might not have seen you, you know. You could just write something like 'I like you' or something like that."

"Oh yes! That's a good idea. Can I do it right now?" Becky asked.

"As soon as you're finished rinsing those carrots, you sure can take a break and do it," Mom answered.

A few minutes later, Becky had left the kitchen and was busily drawing a card for Jonathan in the living room. Janet, looking at Mom, said, "You would think she would have noticed that his legs were messed up! I noticed that right away."

"Yes, but we all have to learn things the first time, Janet," Mom reminded her. "That's probably the first person she ever remembers seeing who was very different from her. We can't expect her just to automatically understand things, you know. Now, let's get these carrots finished so we can start lunch for the hay workers. I'm sure they're going to be hungry in a few minutes!"

Meanwhile, out in the hay loft, Sarah and Ben were busy unloading a wagon of hay. It was hot, dusty work and both were glad that the lunch bell would be ringing soon. Still, it was neat to see the bales of hay quickly filling the loft area and know that this was God's provision of food for the cows this winter. Although it was exhausting, Sarah nearly always felt a sense of extreme satisfaction and accomplishment when the hay was finally safely in the barn.

"Did you hear that Luke Williams is coming for a visit next weekend, Sarah?" asked Ben, not stopping from throwing bales to make this query.

"Yes, I think that will be nice," answered Sarah. "It must be so lonely to be away from your family and not know many people where you live. I'm sure at least he won't be lonely here!" Then after a pause to wipe her forehead, she continued, "He seems like a nice boy. Does he get along well with Jeff?"

"Yes," said Ben, "but then again, Luke seems to get along well with everyone. He can be so funny. But not the 'make-fun-of-somebody' funny if you know what I mean. He seems nice. I think," he said, looking at Sarah, "that . . ."

Ben never had a chance to finish his sentence. A voice from below broke in. "Come on down, you two!" Dad called. "Let's get some water to drink and see if lunch is about ready." Jeff and Dad were obviously ready to take a much-needed break.

Chapter Twenty

*I*t was the last Sunday of September. Sarah, sitting in church before the service began, was having trouble getting her mind ready to worship.

For some reason, she was distracted easily. It might be due to the rushing around she had to do to help get everyone ready for church.

As she looked to her right Sarah saw James sitting with his family. It seemed almost impossible not to think about how things might have been if courtship had occurred. That was strange because it had been several months since Sarah had such thoughts. If the truth were told, these thoughts were not all good or bad.

Sarah wondered if he would have revealed a tender side to his personality. What if he had actually displayed signs of affection for the children? Surely, she hoped, some of the examples Jeff set would have had some kind of impact on him. In fact, even if the courtship did not end in marriage, it was possible that he might have matured. But there were those other things about James, things her father could not share with Sarah. No, it was good that James had not courted her. She trusted Dad completely.

She glanced back around to look at her own family members and at Dad specifically. As she did so, her gaze passed by Luke. Luke had been visiting with her family since Friday evening and was now attending church with them. He was sitting up straight with a determined look on his face. It was as though he planned on catching every single word that the preacher was going to say. Sarah turned her own full attention to the preacher as the service began.

Indeed, Luke had arrived Friday night with the usual anxious watchfulness of the smaller children. Becky and Rachel started to look out the windows every few minutes at 1:00, even though Mom had said that Luke couldn't possibly be expected until after 6:00 or 6:30. "But," said Becky with her usual enthusiasm, "you can just never tell! He might come early, Mommy, and we don't want to miss seeing him get here." Why is it that small children get so excited about company? It's probably just that the rest of us have already experienced it so often that the novelty is gone. Regardless, Becky and Rachel kept their faithful vigil up for six hours or so before Luke finally arrived.

The visit by Luke up to this point didn't really include anything unusual or particularly noteworthy. Luke helped do the chores Friday night after he arrived. He went to bed early, around 9:00, and was up at 5:00 the next morning. "I have always liked to get up early," he said. "It just makes me feel I can get more done during the day."

On Saturday, Luke worked hard with Jeff and Dad mending barbed wire fences along the roadway, and building a new feed bin. Miscalculating once while swinging his hammer, the hammer's head came crashing down on two fingers of his left hand. Luke didn't say anything, but he did take the hammer and slam it very hard into the board he was working on. Just one time, but it was obviously done as some way for him to relieve his anger and pay the hammer back for causing him pain. He didn't say anything about it and neither did Jeff or Dad. By supper they had the bin almost completely built.

The only time Sarah saw Luke on Saturday was at meals. And there, he was quiet and not assertive. She noticed that he didn't ask lots of questions and demand the "table's attention" like some guests did. He was friendly, smiled a lot, and responded to any questions directed to him.

Actually, Luke seemed to give most of his table attention to Becky and Rachel. He had asked if it were possible for him to sit between the two little girls at meals. A few times at meals, the two girls would suddenly start giggling, because of something that Luke did for them or said to them.

On Saturday evening, Luke had retired again around 9 p.m. Before he did, though, he found an opportunity to speak with Jeff and Dad for a few minutes in private. "I would like to apologize for hitting my hammer on that board in anger today," he said, looking down at the blood blisters that had formed on his injured fingers.

"I understand," said Jeff. "Sometimes when I get hurt badly, I want to cram my fist through the wall to take my mind off the pain and to relieve my anger." He added, "If I do hit something, that ends up hurting worse than the original injury!"

"But that's not the way I want to act," Luke said. "I need to keep my emotions in check and not act or think out of control. I'm afraid I work with a few pretty rough characters sometimes and their example rubs off on me, instead of mine rubbing off on them." After a moment, Luke added, "My boss, Evan Taylor, is a fine Christian man, and he has been trying to help me see the way that a Christian should respond to pain or injury. Anyway, I apologize to you both for the bad example I set."

"We'll pray for you," said Dad. "And you keep us in your prayers too, okay? We all struggle with anger and wrong reactions at times."

So that is how the weekend had progressed up to church on Sunday. On the way home from church, the family members were chattering about what they had learned and who they had talked to. After a minute, Luke complimented the preacher. But not in a flattering, "butter-up-the-McLeans" kind of way. It was just a comment that he genuinely meant. He said, "I like the way your preacher uses scripture a lot. Too often it's easy to get caught up in interesting stories or examples from today's world. That's not wrong, by itself. But everything your preacher said had a scriptural basis." It was obvious that Luke held God's Word in high regard.

After lunch on Sunday, Becky and Rachel were pretending to make a meal in one corner of the kitchen. Sarah was helping with dishes and noticed what occurred when Luke and Jeff walked through. Luke, seeing what the girls were doing, stopped in his tracks.

"Say, can a fellow get something good to eat here, girls?" Luke asked. "I sure am hungry and that spaghetti looks good. Mind if I have a bite?"

"It's meat loaf and french fries. Yes, you can

eat," replied Becky a little sheepishly, "if you want to."

"Why of course I want to!" said Luke. "It's not every day that a man gets to eat a good meal like that! It smells so good, too." He sat right down on the floor and pretended to eat.

Sarah had often pretended to eat these imitation meals. So had everyone in the family. Then what made Luke's pretending to eat with the girls so different or special?

She kept working and then it dawned on her. It was because Luke so proactively sought to pretend with them. He didn't have to be coaxed or begged by the girls. Also, he didn't seem in a hurry to leave the floor. He was really having fun.

Late in the afternoon it started to look like rain. Sure enough by 4:00 the rain started. It got cooler also. Rachel called it "really cold." At about that time, Luke said goodbye and thanked everyone for their kindness and hospitality. To Sarah he said, "Thanks for the wonderful meals you made, Sarah. They were great." That had been about the extent of his conversation with her during the weekend.

After he left, Becky and Rachel sort of moped around the house. In fact, so did Jeff and Ben. It could have been blamed on the weather. Cold rain can take the good spirits out of just about anyone. But Sarah thought it was in large part due to Luke's departure.

Funny. Sarah felt just a little sad that he was gone also. It seemed funny because she hadn't really spent any time with him at all. Just the meals. But he was one of those guests that naturally makes everyone a little sad when they leave.

"He sure is a nice young man. I hope he can come back for a visit soon," she found herself thinking as she was dropping off to sleep. After a few moments of what can only be described as more concentrated thought, her mind echoed itself, ". . . real soon, I hope."

Chapter Twenty-one

Over the next several months, Luke became a frequent visitor to the McLeans' home. About every other weekend, an observer would have been able to find two little girls, staring out the windows on Friday afternoon, chattering about their friend Luke. When he arrived, it was hard to know who was happier, the two little girls or the young man who walked through the front door. But it really didn't matter. No one was keeping score anyway!

On Saturday mornings after breakfast, Luke would usually say something like, "Well, I sure hope you have a lot of things I can help with on the farm today. If I'm going to eat your fine cooking, which I do intend to do wholeheartedly, then I need to earn my keep! What are we going to work on today, Jeff?"

And work they did. They cut, hauled, and split firewood; repaired things that inevitably break in a barn; and even dug out and replaced a part of the buried water pipe that had frozen on a cold night. Jeff and Luke always came laughing into the kitchen at lunch-time with appetites that were uncommonly large!

Meal times continued to be fun ones for the whole family. Luke, after being encouraged by Dad, began to tell stories of growing up in the Williams' home. Many were funny, but some were sad. Luke, always remembering that he had young ears in his audience, made sure the little girls understood what he was talking about. Questions like, "Do you know what that means?" or "Does that make sense to you, Becky?" were frequently asked by Luke. And he made sure that anything scary was not too scary for little ears. He didn't want them afraid at night thinking about something that had happened a long time ago.

Once he told about how his little sister Hope had "helped" check for eggs. "We had about 25 laying hens at that time and no one had checked for eggs all day. Hope must have been about five years old, and she decided she was old enough to bring in those eggs by herself. She reached in to grab an egg, but one of the chickens pecked her in protest. It didn't hurt her, but she decided she wouldn't let it happen again. To make sure, she opened the door to the chicken coop and shooed all 25 hens and the rooster right out of there!" He paused.

"Then what happened?" Becky asked quickly, laughing at the thought of chickens running loose everywhere.

"Well, it sure made it easier to get the eggs. Since the coop was so nice and empty she decided while she was in there to clean up the chickens' droppings. That's a messy job for anybody, as you know, but it was especially messy for a little girl who could barely hold the shovel. Needless to say, she didn't make much progress on cleaning up the coop but she did get herself pretty filthy!

"Then she remembered about the eggs, and quickly gathered them. I guess maybe she was starting to feel like she was doing things she shouldn't be doing. Anyway, she picked up the eggs, probably about twenty of them, nestled them in her dress, and headed to the house."

"I've done that!" exclaimed Becky.

"I'm sure you have. And it can be a good way to bring in the eggs, too. But what Hope didn't realize is that Jonathan had left his bike in the middle of the path. She didn't see it and tripped on the handlebars. When she did every one of those eggs broke into a million pieces, and everything inside those eggs flooded all over her dress. When she stood up the 'egg goop' ran down her legs and into her shoes.

"Now Hope isn't one to get discouraged very easily. Instead of bursting into tears, she ran into the kitchen, leaving a trail of 'egg goop' everywhere she walked. Mom saw her and exclaimed, 'Hope, what happened to you?'

"Hope, not the least bit embarrassed, looked at Mom and announced, 'I got the eggs, Mommy!' 'I see you did!' said Mom. And then, Hope, using the most grown-up voice she could, said, 'And Mommy, I think I'm old enough to get them every day.'"

Everyone laughed, even the little girls. It was stories like that Mom and Dad loved to hear. It made them feel like they were getting "caught up" on what had happened to Mark and Carol in past years.

Luke became such a frequent visitor that the family set up a bed for him in the boys' room. It was their way of expressing how welcome he was at their home. The little girls rarely argued, but one area of contention for them was deciding who was going to get to change his sheets and get the bed ready for Luke on Friday morning.

"It's my time, you did it for him last visit!" Becky might say to Rachel. "Oh, no! I remember! I remember that you did. Because I said to myself that next time it would be my turn!" would be the reply by Rachel. Mom tried using these squalls as a way to teach the little girls to give up their own wishes and please the other person. This would sometimes backfire, with one little girl saying, "Okay, you do it. Really, it's okay. I want you to get to do it," followed by the other girl saying, "No, I really want you to get to do it. It will be fun for you, so you just do it. I don't care." Although this conflict also had to be resolved, it was at least moving the girls in the right direction!

One Saturday morning Jeff came into the kitchen and spoke quietly to Sarah. "I just had the strangest thing happen with Luke," he said. "I was going up to my room to get another pair of wool socks and there sat Luke on his bed." He paused, which gave Sarah enough time to reply, "That doesn't sound strange, Jeff. Now, if he were sitting on the ceiling, that would be strange."

Jeff smiled, "That's not all. He was looking, no, staring would be a better way to put it . . . he was staring at this little piece of paper in his hand. When I came in, it took him a second to realize I was in there, and then he quickly slid the piece of paper into his pocket. His face turned a little red, and he just said something like, 'So, is it time to do chores?' Now, doesn't that sound strange to you? Why didn't he tell me what was on that piece of paper? Why was he embarrassed? And why was he staring at it so intently?

It was almost like he was . . . well, kind of worshiping it or something."

"Jeff, you're something, did you know that?" Sarah laughed. "I don't have a clue what he was looking at, but why does it seem so strange? It could be a letter from his parents. It could be a list of things he needs to buy at the store when he returns. It could be the tag that he just pulled off his shirt! I hardly think looking at a piece of paper is grounds for calling someone 'strange.'"

"I didn't call him strange. I just said it seemed strange the way he acted," Jeff replied a little defensively. "You would be wondering the same thing if you had seen it the way I did. I wonder what he was looking at."

"Well, I hope I wouldn't be wondering," Sarah replied. "I hope I would just consider it none of my business and go on about my life." Then she added, with a touch of compassion in her voice, "I must admit that I am often curious also, Jeff. I guess it's just human nature. But I wouldn't think about this much more if I were you."

"You're probably right," Jeff admitted, "you usually are, you know. Still, I can't help wondering, . . ." he said quietly as he left the kitchen and walked out the door.

Later that morning, Luke was walking with Jeff in the woods by the house. They were talking about the way the air felt so crisp and clean on cold early winter days, when Luke suddenly changed the subject.

"Your sister Sarah sure is a nice girl," he said.

"Does she always make meals as well as she does on the weekends?"

Jeff laughed. "I guess I've never thought about the variance in meals she makes. They all taste good to me! I've heard Dad say to Mom, though, that God has given Sarah an unusual ability in cooking. She almost never forgets to add all the ingredients (which I wish could also be said about Janet!), almost never gets flustered if it's a complicated meal or lots of things come out of the oven at the same time, and just really seems to like doing it. She's made a lot of meals for families in our church when someone gets sick or dies." He added, "Yes, she's a good cook. I don't think she cooks any differently on the weekends, though. Why?"

"Oh, just curious I guess," Luke replied, quickly changing the subject again. "Did you see that? Looked kind of like a pheasant, didn't it?"

"I didn't see it. It flew away too fast," Jeff answered, glancing in the direction Luke was pointing. The talk about food had aroused an interest in what Sarah might be preparing for lunch. "I wonder what we're having for lunch? Did you notice?"

"Well, I did see Sarah slicing some carrots and potatoes," Luke replied. "But I don't know what they were for."

"Maybe we should be heading back. Sure would hate to miss the dinner bell, if you know what I mean," Jeff said, turning toward the house. Suddenly, Jeff remembered the mysterious incident with Luke and the paper. He wanted so badly to ask about it, but Sarah's words kept coming back to him. It really was none of his business.

Almost as if reading Jeff's thoughts, Luke began, "I guess you saw what I was doing up in the bedroom this morning. I feel kind of embarrassed about it. It's not like I couldn't let you see, you know."

Jeff didn't know what to say. Apparently, Luke must have thought that Jeff saw more than he actually did. "I didn't see what you were looking at. Besides, it's really not any of my business, Luke."

"Jeff, you're a sharp guy. Most guys would have come right out and asked what I was looking at. I appreciate your constraint."

Jeff was feeling guilty. He hadn't really wanted to exhibit constraint. In fact, if Sarah hadn't said what she said . . .

But before Jeff could express his thoughts, Luke continued, "That paper had a Bible verse on it. I'm trying to memorize Bible passages and I'm afraid I have a lot of trouble doing it! I don't think I am stupid or anything, I just have this mental block or something that makes it hard for me to memorize Bible verses. Maybe it's Satan making it hard for me. I didn't want you to see, because I'm embarrassed about my handicap. Too, I don't want to appear to be putting on airs or acting like 'I am good. I'm memorizing Bible verses,' or anything."

Jeff was excited about his new-found knowledge of Luke. He had been secretly fearing that Luke had some problem or sin he was trying to hide. "Why is it," Jeff thought, "that we often think the worst about someone when we don't have all the facts?" Even for someone who had proven himself as much as Luke had!

"Luke, you've just helped me commit to learn more verses myself. I'm afraid I don't make it much of a priority in my life. And I'll pray that God would bless your efforts. I know He will! Hey, let's run home, okay? I'm getting cold. Besides, we might get to sink our teeth into lunch sooner."

"Let's go!" shouted Luke, and they were off.

Nor were walks with Luke confined to just Jeff. Over the weeks, everyone got to take at least one walk with Luke, even the little girls. Mom and Dad took several walks with Luke, late in November, and when they returned home Mom and Dad seemed in a particularly good mood. Mostly, however, Luke's walk companion was Jeff. Occasionally, Janet and/or Sarah would also join the pair. These walks were especially delightful for Janet, who seemed to think the world of Luke.

Sarah also enjoyed these walks quite a lot. At first, she was afraid she would be a little jealous of not getting to take a walk with just her brother Jeff, as she often did. However, she learned on her first walk that she actually enjoyed having Luke's perspective on the topics they discussed. No, she didn't mind taking walks with Jeff and Luke at all.

It was on a walk that Sarah took with Luke and Jeff, during Luke's last visit before Christmas, that Jeff brought up a new topic. "Say Luke, what do you think you'll be doing this next year? Are you going to keep working for Evan Taylor, or do you think you'll branch out on your own? And have you given thought as to where you might set up for business if you do decide that is the way to go?"

Luke seemed a little embarrassed by the question. "Oh, I am praying about that and asking God to show me His will for my life."

"Yes," persisted Jeff, "but surely you have some ideas about what you'll be doing next year. What are your plans?"

For some reason, Luke didn't answer Jeff's question right away. Instead he looked off and watched a squirrel playing and chattering in a nearby tree. He sighed softly, then turned to Jeff and said, "I'll just have to wait and see, Jeff. Evan has plenty of work to keep me busy, that's for sure. But in terms of what I'll do next year, I can't say. I have a lot of decisions to make. I do miss my family and the ability to talk to my parents and brothers and sisters a lot. I'll just have to wait and see."

That answer seemed to satisfy Jeff, because he didn't follow up with any more questions. In fact, the mood of the trio was quite subdued. It was as if each of the three was thinking about their own futures and what God had in store for them.

As Luke prepared to leave late that afternoon, many acts of kindness and love were expressed. Becky and Rachel had made Luke a painting, and they presented it to him with a great deal of gravity and emotion. Rachel, acting as the spokesman for the two said, "We made this for you. We're going to miss seeing you. You are going to come back after Christmas, aren't you?"

"I sure hope so," Luke said with feeling. He gave them both a big hug. Sarah noticed tears forming in Luke's eyes as he put Becky back down.

"Be sure and tell your parents 'hi' for us," Mom said, and Dad echoed.

Jeff, Janet, Ben, and Steve also came by Luke's room as he was packing up to say goodbye. Sarah knew she should say goodbye, but for some reason it was hard to walk up to the boys' room where everyone had gathered. She realized how much she had learned to enjoy Luke's visits. Finally, telling herself she was just being silly, she did walk to where the others were standing. "I do hope you have a safe trip. Please take care and tell your Mom and Dad 'hi' from me. I hope you'll be able to come back in January."

"Thanks," Luke said. "I'm sure I'll be back in January."

As Luke walked out the door, Dad said, "Let's make some popcorn and then sing Christmas carols!" All of the older ones knew that he was trying to cheer up the family and went along with it. Soon, everyone seemed to be happier, and before long it was time for bed.

As Sarah settled down for sleep, she thought she heard Rachel crying softly in her bed. Walking over close to her bed, Sarah saw that Rachel was crying indeed. "What's the matter, honey?"

"I miss Luke. And I'm afraid it'll be a long time before we see him again."

"I know," Sarah found herself telling Rachel, "I miss him a lot too. But he will be back if it's God's will." Then she added reassuringly, "I think he'll be back."

After settling Rachel, Sarah lay back down. As she drifted off to sleep, she whispered once more ". . . if it's God's will."

Chapter Twenty-two

"He's home! He's home!" Suddenly, the house seemed to come alive as boys, girls, and parents ran to the front door. Luke heard the shouts from outside the house and shouted back, "Yes, I'm home!"

The door flew open and more arms were reaching for him than could possibly belong to just nine people. In characteristic fashion, his little sisters, Beth, Hope, and Anna, all started talking at once trying to tell him everything that had happened in the house for the last three and a half months. Not to be outdone, and not accustomed to their brother being gone so long, his brothers, Jonathan and Matthew, chimed in, giving their account of the latest news at the Williams' house.

Demonstrating more maturity and self-control, it was later that Daniel and Andrew filled him in on other details about home. They also had more questions for him. "What is it like to work for Mr. Taylor? Do you have fun on your new job? Who does your laundry and mends your clothes? Have you visited with the McLeans since your last letter? What do you do at their house?" So many questions, but so much time to answer them all. Luke was planning to stay home for the next four days before returning to his carpentry job.

That evening, he did chores with his brothers. Chores with his brothers! Although he had never realized it, he had really missed this. Work is never so hard or so bad when you do it with someone you love. Their conversations continued.

"Do you do chores at the McLeans when you visit them?" asked Jonathan.

Although he remembered detailing his activities at the McLeans in many letters home, Luke still answered his brother's question with kindness. "I sure do," he said. "They have a bigger operation than we do. I've learned some things I want to share with Dad that might work here also. Of course, that will be his decision to make."

Later, after the chores were done, Luke asked for everyone to gather in the living room. When they were seated, he left the room for a moment and came back, carrying his suitcase.

"What's in that?" asked Beth excitedly.

"Well, I guess we'll just have to open it and see, won't we?" answered Luke smiling. He opened up the luggage and distributed gifts to each person.

"Are these Christmas gifts?" asked Matthew.

"No, they are just friendship gifts," said Luke. As each person opened his or her package, they realized that the gifts were from the McLean family members. Becky had sent a homemade handkerchief to Beth. Rachel sent Hope three beautiful rocks she had found. "How pretty!" exclaimed Hope.

Everyone else opened their small gifts, all of which were handmade or something the McLean children had found on their farm. "It was a beautiful thought to send these gifts," Mom said. "It makes me feel less like I've not seen you these last months, for some reason."

"Can we send them some presents too?" asked Daniel hopefully. "Luke can take them back with him when he visits them again. You will be seeing them again soon, won't you?"

"I hope so," Luke said. Changing the subject, he reached into his luggage again and said, "Hey, there's something else in here." With that he pulled out a small set of packages for his brothers and sisters. These were gifts from Luke himself. Tears and hugs were shared freely as Luke's family realized that he had never, not even for one day, forgotten them.

"What about us?" laughed his dad. "Where's our present? Didn't you find some way to carry a cow home in that luggage of yours?"

"Now, Mark," scolded Mom, laughing, "just having Luke home is our present."

"I didn't forget you," said Luke laughing. "I'll give you yours later."

It was one of those nights when parents think their children will never settle down and go to sleep. Beth must have gotten up three times for more water, and one more hug from Luke. Jonathan came down and said he just remembered something he forgot to tell Luke and just had to tell him right now! After about an hour, the trips downstairs slowed and then stopped completely. It seemed that all of the younger children were finally asleep. After awhile, Andrew, Daniel, and Matthew also got drowsy and decided to head to bed.

Then Mom said, "Although I'm glad you're home Luke, if I don't go to bed soon, I won't be able to see you tomorrow because I'll sleep all day." With a gentle hug for Luke and a look of gratitude in her eyes that God had brought her boy back home, she turned and went upstairs to bed.

It was very quiet in the house. Luke was so thankful to be back home and be with his family again. How he thanked God for his love for them. He looked over at Dad and saw a questioning look in his eyes. However, Dad didn't say anything.

After awhile, Luke said, "Dad, I've got some important things to talk to you about. I would wait until tomorrow if I could, but I don't think that's possible. Do you think you could stay up a few more minutes?"

"Yes, Luke," answered his dad. "I knew you had something on your mind. You're my boy, and I know you pretty well."

"Dad, I've spent a lot of time in prayer about something. I've thought about it and now I need to ask your advice." It was so easy and natural for Luke to talk to his dad. He didn't feel nervous at all.

"Dad, I have decided that I want to court Sarah McLean," Luke said after a slight pause. "I am seeking your permission to do so."

His dad rose quickly from his seat and gave his son a big hug. "I'm so happy that you have sought God's will in this matter. Sarah comes from a fine family. I respect David and Kate probably more than anyone I know. I will want to pray about it and talk to your mom about it also. You understand don't you? I know of no reason why you can't court her, but we want to make sure this is God's will."

"I understand, Dad," Luke said, "and wouldn't want it any other way. I'm counting on you and Mom to help me make sure I'm doing the right thing, and that I'm doing God's will."

"Let's pray about it right now," said Dad. Dad led in a prayer, thanking God for supplying a potential marriage partner for Luke. He asked God to give him and all parties involved wisdom to make the right decision. He ended by asking God to keep Luke pure and holy throughout the process.

After another hug and a slap on the back, Dad went up to bed. Luke didn't think that anyone in the world was blessed with a better dad.

The next evening, Dad got Luke aside by himself and called for Mom to come into the room. After they were seated, he began.

"Luke, I told Mom of your wish to court Sarah McLean." At this, his conversation ceased while Mom jumped up and hugged her son of 21 years. Then Dad continued, "We've prayed about it and feel that the Lord is leading us to be with Sarah a short time. That doesn't mean that we have any serious doubts. In fact, we can't think of any reason why you shouldn't court her. But we don't know her well, and would like to spend some time with her first. Do you understand?"

"Yes," said Luke. "Like I said last night, I view your role as helpers in this process, not as a hinderer."

"Well, here's what we're thinking. You'll be going back to work in a few days. What if our family goes along with you and we spend a day with the McLean family again? We wouldn't have to say anything about this situation. We are just good friends and would like to see them again. Besides, our children are wanting to see their children again anyway. While we are there we can observe Sarah. What do you think? Does it seem wise to you?"

"I think it's a great idea, Dad," Luke said warmly. "Oh, Dad and Mom, I know you are just going to love her."

"I think so too," said Mom. "Now, we better start making our plans and getting things together. We're going to take a trip!"

In a few days, the Williams indeed took a visit to the McLeans. It was a wonderful visit, just like the one they had a few months earlier. Only this time, the children already knew each other and starting having fun from the very first minute.

The Williams observed Sarah closely, without calling attention to the fact. What they saw was a sweet, kind, obedient daughter whose love was in the Lord Jesus Christ. When Mark talked to David about Sarah, he learned that everything they saw was indeed fact.

As the visit came to a close, the McLeans and Williams said good-bye. "I hope we can see each other again soon," said David McLean.

"I wouldn't be surprised," was Mark Williams' interesting reply.

That night Luke's Mom and Dad had a brief conversation with Luke. "You have our permission and our blessing to court Sarah McLean," said Dad. "I feel that God is leading in this. It's so exciting. We will keep you in our prayers daily." Then with a prayer and hugs of joy they all went to bed.

Chapter Twenty-three

*M*id-January was cold. Even the old timers commented about the weather; "bitterly cold" they announced it to be. Wood piles set aside for wood-burning furnaces made rapid declines. Even the few birds which stayed in the area for the winter seemed to sing colder, somehow.

Life on the McLean farm was made more difficult by the bitterly cold environment. Cows had to be fed more often. Their water tanks, which had to be broken up many times each day by Jeff, would start to freeze back just as soon as Jeff turned his back and headed to the warmth of the house.

Inside, the house was warm, but everything had a different hue to it. Practically every inch of every window was so caked with frost, and stayed that way continuously, that they were useless as a means of looking outside. In some ways that was a blessing. The sunshine seemed almost too intense, because the snow-covered landscape had turned to a brightly reflective sheet of ice.

Even though it was cold, a listener outside a window of the McLean home would have perhaps been surprised to hear the happy sounds of laughter. No one seemed to be suffering the effects of cabin fever, even though they had been pretty much closed in for the last week and a half. Why this happy mood? The reason was approaching the house at that very minute.

Luke, wrapped up in several layers of coats, mufflers, hats, and gloves, was approaching the front door. Someone inside squealed and soon the door was flung open wide, as if saying to the cold, "Yes cold, you can come in for a minute. Just as long as you bring Luke in with you!"

It was a few minutes before Luke could speak. First, he had to uncover enough layers to find his mouth. He had lots of little hands helping him do that. Then he had to get his mouth warmed up and working again.

"Did you girls know it's a little bit cold out-side?" asked Luke.

"Yes!" replied Becky and Rachel in unison, followed by a long listing of all of the things that had frozen, or were affected by the cold.

"Such trouble!" said Luke. "Well, it's a good thing I'm here. Maybe I can help Jeff. Where is he anyway?"

"He just came in from the barn," Sarah replied, walking into the foyer just as Luke asked his question. "Welcome back."

"Thanks," said Luke. "My, it sure is good to see you." Then he looked from Sarah to the little girls. "You, too," he said, and picked up first one and then the other in his strong arms.

After supper, Luke chose a time when no one was nearby and asked David McLean if he could speak with him in private for a few moments. "Sure," David replied. "Why don't we go into the living room? It doesn't look like anyone is in there right now. We better do it before it fills up with people, though," he added, laughing.

When they were seated, Luke began. "Mr. McLean, I have prayed about something for a long time and feel like now is the time I am supposed to share this with you. Sir, I would like to ask your permission to court Sarah. I have discussed this with my parents and, after much prayer and discussion, they have given not only their permission but their blessing. I am serious about my desire to court your daughter. If, after courting her, I continue to find her to be God's choice for my wife, it is my intention to ask her to marry me."

"Luke, I'm so happy that you have taken an interest in Sarah. I think God has been preparing her for these last twenty years for such a godly man as yourself. As you know, I will need to discuss this with Mrs. McLean and pray about it before I can give you my decision. I'll try to let you know before the weekend is over, though."

"Thank you, sir," Luke said. "I appreciate that."

For the next thirty minutes or so Dad asked Luke a number of direct questions related to Luke's views and beliefs. Since Dad had spent so much time with Luke these last few months, he already knew the answers to most of them and they were able to make fast progress. Dad closed the session with a prayer.

That evening, Dad shared Luke's request with Mom. She cried, then laughed for pure joy, then cried some more. She had felt for quite some time that Luke would make an ideal mate for Sarah. In fact, so had Dad. They had been gathering information about his beliefs and views for quite a while now. And just a few weeks ago, Dad had asked Mark Williams a number of questions about his son, Luke. Dad and Mom prayed and asked God to give them wisdom and help them know when to announce their decision. Before they went to sleep, they were convinced that they should give Luke their permission to court Sarah.

Early Saturday morning found Sarah busily cleaning up in the kitchen. "Sarah, can you come into the living room for a minute please?" Dad asked.

"Luke has asked permission to court you, Sarah. Your mother and I have prayed about this and feel we can give not only our permission, but our blessing as well. Before I talk to Luke, though, I want to know if that is your wish also."

"Yes, Dad, it is my wish," she broke down crying. Tears of joy and relief. She had not told anyone about how the Lord had been impressing upon her for quite some time that Luke should be her husband. After a few minutes of hugging her dad, she continued, "I've prayed about this already and know that God wants me to take this step, Dad. When are you going to tell him?" she asked excitedly.

"Well, there is no time like the present I suppose! I'll go find him and be right back in." Dad disappeared with a big smile on his face and a decided spring in his step. In a few minutes he walked back into the living room, with Luke following along behind. Luke seemed surprised to find Sarah standing there.

Dad did not make Luke wait to hear his answer. "Luke, you have our permission and our blessing to court Sarah. We would love to have you as our son-in-law if that is God's will. Sarah has agreed that she would like you to court her, also." Dad was positively beaming! But, then again, so was everyone else in the room.

For a second it was a little awkward. Sarah didn't know what to do or say and neither did Luke. Dad saved the day, though, by stating, "Let's all go into the kitchen and celebrate. Kate, why don't you mix up some kind of treat? And Sarah, why don't you get us all some glasses of cold milk? Luke and I will... well, we'll stand by in case you need assistance!... Oh, and we'll clean up the dishes, too," he added, winking at Mom.

It was a wonderful weekend for Sarah. She and Luke began talking more about their beliefs and their dreams. Often they would sit and talk in the kitchen as Sarah prepared meals. Sarah felt really comfortable talking to Luke, and knew he felt the same way.

On Saturday afternoon, Luke and Sarah took a walk with Jeff and Janet, who walked about fifteen feet in front of them, talking to each other. After a few minutes, Sarah asked Luke, "Do you want to be a church leader someday? Have you thought about being an elder or a deacon?"

"Well," Luke replied, "I have thought about it some. I've studied the qualifications for both offices. I feel so unworthy to hold either one right now. Some of the character traits that are mentioned are the things I find myself asking God to help me mature in each day." He paused, then continued, "But I suppose it's not my decision anyway. If God leads the church I am worshiping with to ask me to serve, I am willing to do His will. I would never try and get people to think about me or vote for me, though. I feel it should be the Holy Spirit leading his people to choose the right person."

Sarah reflected that this answer showed a great deal of maturity and thought on Luke's part. She had known of men who seemed to 'campaign' for the job of elder and it just didn't seem right to her. On the other hand, she had known of men who had been chosen by the church to serve, but refused to serve because they didn't think they had the time. It seemed to her that Luke's perspective was the right one.

All too soon the weekend was over and it was time for Luke to head back home. "When will you be back?" asked Sarah hopefully.

"I plan on coming back every other weekend if I can," Luke replied. "I would like to make it every weekend, but the work load just won't allow it. We have been working every other Saturday for half a day to try and get this family's house finished." Then, quietly he added, "I'll miss you."

"And I will miss you," Sarah answered softly.

Luke wrapped up carefully and, with a look of determination on his face, walked into the cold, snowy January landscape.

"God, please help me to be patient," was Sarah's silent prayer as she watched him trudging away.

Chapter Twenty-four

Indeed, Luke was able to visit with the McLeans every other weekend during the winter months. In fact, a pattern of activity almost became the norm. Luke would arrive on Friday night, and spend time talking with Sarah's family. On Saturday, Luke continued helping with chores and projects that were underway in the morning. In the afternoon, he and Sarah would spend time together talking about things important to their lives. These talks were always arranged by Luke so that one or more of Sarah's family members were somewhere nearby. On Saturday evening, Luke and Sarah would do whatever the family was doing. Sometimes it was singing and telling stories. Other evenings it was making popcorn. Whatever, Luke always seemed to fit right in. On Sundays, the family would go to church. On Sunday afternoons, again Sarah and Luke had time for conversation. Sarah thought she had never had so much fun in her life as she experienced on the weekends when Luke came to visit.

On a walk around the hay field one cold, February Saturday afternoon, Sarah suddenly stopped and turned to Luke. "Luke, what if I displease you?"

"What do you mean?" Luke said, laughing. "How are you planning on displeasing me? Do you have some tricks up your sleeve that you haven't told me about yet?"

"I'm serious, Luke," Sarah said, smiling. "What if something I do is not what you want me to do? What if I cook something wrong or not the way your Mom would have cooked it? What if I want to continue some Thanksgiving traditions that my family started, but you really don't like? I don't know what it might be. But what would you do?"

"It's a little hard to answer without knowing what it might be we're talking about, Sarah," Luke answered. "I hope it won't happen often. In fact, I think we can help avoid having it happen by just talking about things a lot. Communicating with each other. We've got to do that, you know. We should never just clam up and not tell the other person what we're thinking or feeling."

After more reflection, Luke continued, "I suppose it would depend on what it is, like I said. If it was a minor thing, I would hope I could just let it go and not make a big deal about it. I shouldn't always demand my way. Being the head of the family doesn't give me a license to selfishly pursue my own interests and desires without thinking of your desires and interests.

"If it were something major, though," he stated, "that I felt should not be happening, I would tell you so. Especially if you were not following God's will in something, like not being willing to discipline our children, then I would have to confront the situation. I could see times when I would have to say 'No' to something you wanted to do, especially if it was contrary to what I felt was God's will for your life."

Sarah thought his answer was good. She

agreed with what he said, yet she still had a question in her mind. It was as though she wanted to bring up every possible situation that might arise and see how he planned to react. Of course, that would be impossible to do. Sure, they could talk about lots of scenarios and potential problems, but she knew that choosing to marry Luke also meant that she was choosing to come under his leadership. Since they couldn't discuss every situation that might arise, she would have to trust. Trusting for the future. How often that had been a problem for her.

On another of Luke's visits, he was helping Sarah do the dishes after supper. He noticed the McLean's checkbook on the table as he lay some plates there. It brought a question to his mind. "Sarah, who do you think should be in charge of paying the bills, keeping the checkbook balanced, and stuff like that? Should it be the husband or the wife?"

Sarah answered, "Dad has always done all of that stuff in our house. I guess I've never really thought about it. How did your parents do it?"

"My mom took care of paying all the bills and keeping up with the checkbook. But my dad set up the budget and had control of what was going to be purchased. It's hard to explain, but it's a system that has worked well for them, I guess."

"Is there some way that you would want to set up things in our home?" Sarah asked Luke.

"I don't know. I would have to think about it some more," he replied. "Would you be willing to keep the checkbook if that seemed to me to make sense?"

"I am willing to do whatever you feel is best. I don't know much about it all, but I can certainly learn," she answered.

The next day as they walked, Luke brought up a tough question. "Sarah, what if we weren't able to have children?"

Sarah was stunned. Did he know of some reason that it would be impossible for God to bless them with children? Children were so important to her! She had been waiting so long for the day in which she could cuddle her own little baby. "What do you mean?" she asked, not able to conceal her fear.

"I just mean, what if God doesn't bless us with children? I don't know why it wouldn't happen, but what if it did? Could you handle it? Would you resent having married me?" he asked.

Sarah was relieved somewhat. Still, she did so want to be a mother. After a few minutes of reflection, she answered, "God is in control of our lives. His will should be done. I would be terribly disappointed, I'm afraid, but would learn to trust in Him. I suppose I would pray about it and see what you thought at that time about adopting children. Would that be a possibility?"

"Of course it would," Luke answered quickly. "I love children too, and would be happy to adopt any children that God brought our way." Then he added, soberly, "Of course, I hope that God could bless us with our own children also."

In late March, the cold weather gave way to a warming trend one Sunday afternoon. Luke and Sarah jumped at the chance to sit on the front porch in the swing. It was so relaxing, just sitting there talking about their hopes and dreams for the future. Although Luke had not asked Sarah to marry him, she felt that God was certainly leading her to accept should he do so. Nothing in their conversations had made her doubt that this was the man God was leading her to marry.

"What do I need to know about you that I don't even know enough to ask? Is there something about you that I should know, but don't know yet?" Luke asked seriously.

Sarah thought for a few minutes before answering. There were a few areas that she wasn't sure Luke knew about in her life. Things she had kind of tried to hide at times. But they weren't really major problems. She thought about answering his question by saying that he knew all about her.

Then she thought about the preacher's sermon she had heard not so long ago. The preacher had taught the importance of being totally honest with someone. He had used a horse as an example and had told his congregation to tell the pros and cons of the horse to a potential buyer. Not to do so, he had said, was the same as not being honest.

Sarah thought some more. Well, this was sure more important than selling any old horse. Yet, she had a fear. What if revealing bad things about her made him decide not to marry her? That would be awful!

Even so, it was just like in the horse example. If revealing bad things about your horse causes the buyer not to want to buy your horse, that's okay. The main thing is that you were honest before the Lord and the person.

"You must have a long list, the way you're thinking about it," said Luke, laughing. He was trying to make her feel more comfortable. Luke started wishing that he hadn't asked the question.

"No, I hope it's not too long," said Sarah smiling. "I must admit I was trying to decide if I should tell you or not. Oh, we have to be honest with each other always, don't we?"

"Yes, we should," he answered. "If it helps, let me tell you some things about me that you might not have noticed. I struggle with anger sometimes. I'm not a wild man or anything like that, but anger is an emotion that comes over me if something bad happens suddenly. I don't brood over things and try not to ever be vindictive. I am asking God to help me with it and have seen some progress lately. I can't help the anger, but I can help the way I respond to it and can try to reduce it quickly."

It was obvious that this admission had been hard for Luke. Continuing, he added, "And the other thing you should know is that I'm afraid I am guilty of pride sometimes when I do a job. I work hard at what I do and when I am finished, I am proud of it. I want others to notice my work and comment on it, too. Again, I'm trying to work on that, but it's hard to change."

Sarah was ashamed that she had hesitated to tell Luke of her faults. Here was a man who was willing to share everything with her. She must learn to do the same. Laughing, she said, "Well, I must admit that one of my problems is that I can't admit that I have any problems! I can be quite a perfectionist at times.

It's like everything must be perfect or I can't be happy. I'm afraid that is especially true of my cooking.

"I also have a problem with trusting God for the future," she continued. "I want to know what is going to happen, exactly how it is going to happen, and make sure everything is going to work out well! I need to trust God more. I'm afraid that problem will spill over into my married life also. I may have a problem trusting my husband on things, too."

Luke was silent for a while. Then he spoke. "I'm glad we shared these things with each other. It's important to be honest in all things. We need to pray for ourselves and each other about these issues."

That was all he said. Sarah wished he had said something more about what she had admitted. Did this make her not a suitable wife for him? Did he have doubts about courting her? Did she state her case, perhaps, a little too bluntly? Maybe she should have told him that these were just minor problems in her life, but that she was making great progress on them. Suddenly, a fear swept over her. "Will this make a difference?" her heart cried.

Luke had to leave soon and as Sarah waved and said good-by, she wondered if she was saying good-bye for more than just the weekend.

The next week seemed to drag by for Sarah. She prayed to God for trust and faith in His will, but it was still hard. The weather turned cold again, which didn't help her spirits any.

The following week, Sarah almost dreaded the coming of Friday evening. What if Luke didn't come? What would he say? She must trust in the Lord!

Friday evening came but Luke did not. The little girls kept up their vigil by the window until bedtime but still Luke didn't show up. "Isn't he coming?" Becky asked Sarah anxiously.

"I don't know," was Sarah's troubled reply.

On Saturday morning, Sarah tried to go about her life as though everything was okay. Mom and Dad sensed her apprehension. Mom, trying to make it a casual comment, said, "Did Luke say he might not be here this weekend?"

"He didn't say," Sarah replied.

"Oh, he's just probably gotten busy building that man's house. I'll bet he will be here next weekend instead."

Sarah wanted to believe that but she just couldn't. Somehow she had convinced herself that Luke wouldn't be coming back again. When someone knocked on the door Saturday afternoon, Sarah didn't even go to see who was there.

"Luke!" cried Ben. "We thought maybe you weren't coming. It's good to see you!"

Sarah didn't know whether to come out of the kitchen or not. She honestly was afraid of the look she might find on Luke's face.

Finally, she entered the living room. Luke started talking immediately. "I'm sorry I'm so late. I had to work on the job this morning. That family needs to get into their house sooner than they thought for some reason, and we've almost been working around the clock on it!"

Sarah was relieved somewhat, but not totally. That evening after supper she and her family enter-

160

tained Luke. There was something different about him, of that she was sure. Maybe he had a couple of bad weeks at work. Oh, how she could hardly wait for their walk tomorrow afternoon.

When Luke asked the next afternoon, "Well, Sarah, are you ready to take a walk?" Sarah found herself reluctantly saying "yes." Why was she so reluctant when she had looked forward to this walk so much? She knew it was because she was afraid of what might happen.

Luke sure did seem different as they started their walk. He was very quiet. He seemed as if he had something weighing heavily on his mind. That certainly didn't give Sarah any more confidence.

Sarah stopped by a low spreading apple tree with branches that the children loved to climb and play on. "Luke, what's wrong?" Sarah finally expressed the question that had been in her mind so long. She didn't think she could wait another second to find out.

"Wrong?" asked Luke, a little surprised. "There's nothing wrong."

"Nothing wrong at all, I hope," Luke added. He walked about twenty more yards and then suddenly stopped, and turned to face Sarah directly.

He drew a deep breath and a smile formed on his face. "Sarah, will you marry me?"

Into her questioning eyes, he quickly added, "I've talked to my parents and your parents and they gave me their blessing."

His eyes were so soft. His voice so calm and loving. She already knew her answer because she felt God had revealed it to her many weeks before. Her parents had also told her that they thought Luke would make a fine husband for her. Looking up into his blue eyes she whispered her answer.

Chapter Twenty-five

"Her wedding day dawned clear and bright," thought Sarah to herself as she awoke early one morning in June. "That's the way it always seemed to work out in all the old-fashioned books I've ever read. Oh well," she reflected with a smile, "real life isn't like a book. God controls the weather and He wanted it to rain today."

Sarah lay quietly in bed for a few minutes, listening to the rain on the window beside her bed. It was a soft, steady rain - the kind that promised to continue off and on all day. No brief sudden shower followed by warm sunshine, not today. Sarah knelt beside her bed in the quiet, still half-dark room. She was grateful for this time alone before the day began.

What an important day - so happy and yet also touched with sadness. This would be the last time she would rise in a room with her younger sisters sleeping around her, the last time she would have breakfast with just her own childhood family. Sarah suddenly realized though, that she must stop dwelling on these thoughts. True, many last things had taken place this week, but wasn't that always true in life?

There was a last meal they had together as a family before Samuel was born, and a last time Mom had read her a bedtime story years ago, and . . . well, the list was endless. This seemed most important because it was today, but all of life would contain firsts and lasts. All of history contained firsts and lasts also - and all of the women before her also had many last things. She, Sarah, was just one more, after all. The world would spin on as always!

And there were many first things to look forward to, coming up very soon! The first meal she would eat as a married woman. The first time she would be called "Mrs. Williams." Sarah smiled at that thought. She would probably think the speaker of those words was referring to her wonderful mother-in-law!

Sarah spent the next few minutes in prayer, thanking God again for His blessing on her life. For her wonderful Christian parents, and loving brothers and sisters. Her prayers then turned to Luke and his family, and the years ahead. She especially asked the Lord for His blessing on her as a new wife, that she might please the Lord in her obedience to her husband.

As Sarah ended her prayer, she rose quietly from her knees. Quickly and silently she dressed and made her bed, then made her way out of the bedroom and down the steps. Working quickly, she mixed up a batch of her family's favorite blueberry muffins, though she doubted that she would be able to eat one. Setting the table, she decided to add scrambled eggs to the menu. Sarah began hearing sounds of stirring in the bedrooms upstairs, and glanced at the clock. Good - everything should be ready by the time her family entered the kitchen.

"Sarah, how nice!" Mom exclaimed as she walked into the room. "Happy wedding day, sweetheart," she added, giving Sarah a hug.

Sarah was grateful that everyone began coming in then, and the usual morning hub-bub began. She had wanted the day to begin in a special way, but now she was beginning to question the wisdom of that. Perhaps it should instead be as normal as possible. Her emotions were going to be pretty mixed up already!

Breakfast went smoothly, however, and the morning flew by. How glad and thankful Sarah was that Luke had the same ideas on weddings as Sarah herself. They both felt that a Christian wedding should be very different from a worldly one, and even different from many of the Christian weddings they had attended in the past. Luke and Sarah wanted to begin their lives together in a simple, quiet way, serving the Lord together, and they wished their wedding to reflect that desire.

Mom, Janet, Sarah, and Carol Williams had spent the day before preparing the food. Cold ham, cheese, and chicken salad were ready to make into sandwiches. Fresh fruit had been made into fruit salad, and two cakes had been baked. With lemonade and water for beverages, the meal was complete. It seemed a bit simple and plain even to Sarah, but Luke was very pleased.

"There will be plenty to eat, Sarah," he assured her. "Everyone will enjoy the time and fellowship together, especially since no long hours have been put into elaborate preparations. Besides," he added, smiling at her doubtful expression, "no one could possibly accuse us of trying to show off, or being wasteful. And a meal like this one won't puff you up with pride," he finished, using one of Becky's favorite expressions. Sarah agreed that it certainly wouldn't!

Then after checking to be sure the little girls

weren't close by, Luke added, "I did break down and buy several flavors of ice cream to go with the cake." At Sarah's surprised look, he turned his hands palms up and shrugged his shoulders. "What could I do, with two sets of big blue eyes pleading with me? They told me how much you like cake with ice cream - I have to start off on the right foot with my two new sisters, don't I?"

"As if you hadn't already!" laughed Sarah, thinking of all the love and kindness Luke had shown to Becky and Rachel since they had met.

So the food was taken care of and put out of mind as the hour for the ceremony approached. Dad, Mr. Williams, Luke and Jeff moved the furniture around a bit in the living room, and added a few extra chairs. The wedding would be witnessed by only the families of Luke and Sarah, including the three living grandparents who had arrived the day before. Friends had been told that they could come by later in the afternoon if they wished to see the new couple, and several were sure to stop by.

About 10:30 a.m., Sarah's pastor arrived. He greeted everyone warmly, then Dad took Luke and the pastor into Sarah's room, where Mom, Sarah, and Luke's parents waited. They all prayed together, and the pastor gave instructions to Luke and Sarah from God's Word, on living as husband and wife in a manner pleasing to the Lord.

Mark and Carol Williams, Luke, and the pastor then departed for the living room, while Mom, Dad, and Sarah exchanged hugs once more. As Mom and Dad left the room to go downstairs, Sarah knelt beside her bed for the second time that morning. Her heart was so full of gratitude to the Lord that she found it difficult to form the words to pray. Asking the Holy Spirit to make intercession for her "with groanings which cannot be uttered," Sarah thanked God for His goodness and mercy to His unworthy servant.

Rising to her feet, Sarah walked joyfully toward the steps and to the new life which awaited her.

Epilogue

*R*achel stood beside the rocking chair, her blue eyes full of delight and wonder. With her face upturned to Sarah's, Rachel asked, "Aren't babies special, Sarah? So sweet and tiny and new?"

"They surely are, Rachel," Sarah replied softly. "New from God's hands to ours," she said, as she bent her head to kiss the new little son in her arms.